Discovering Eden

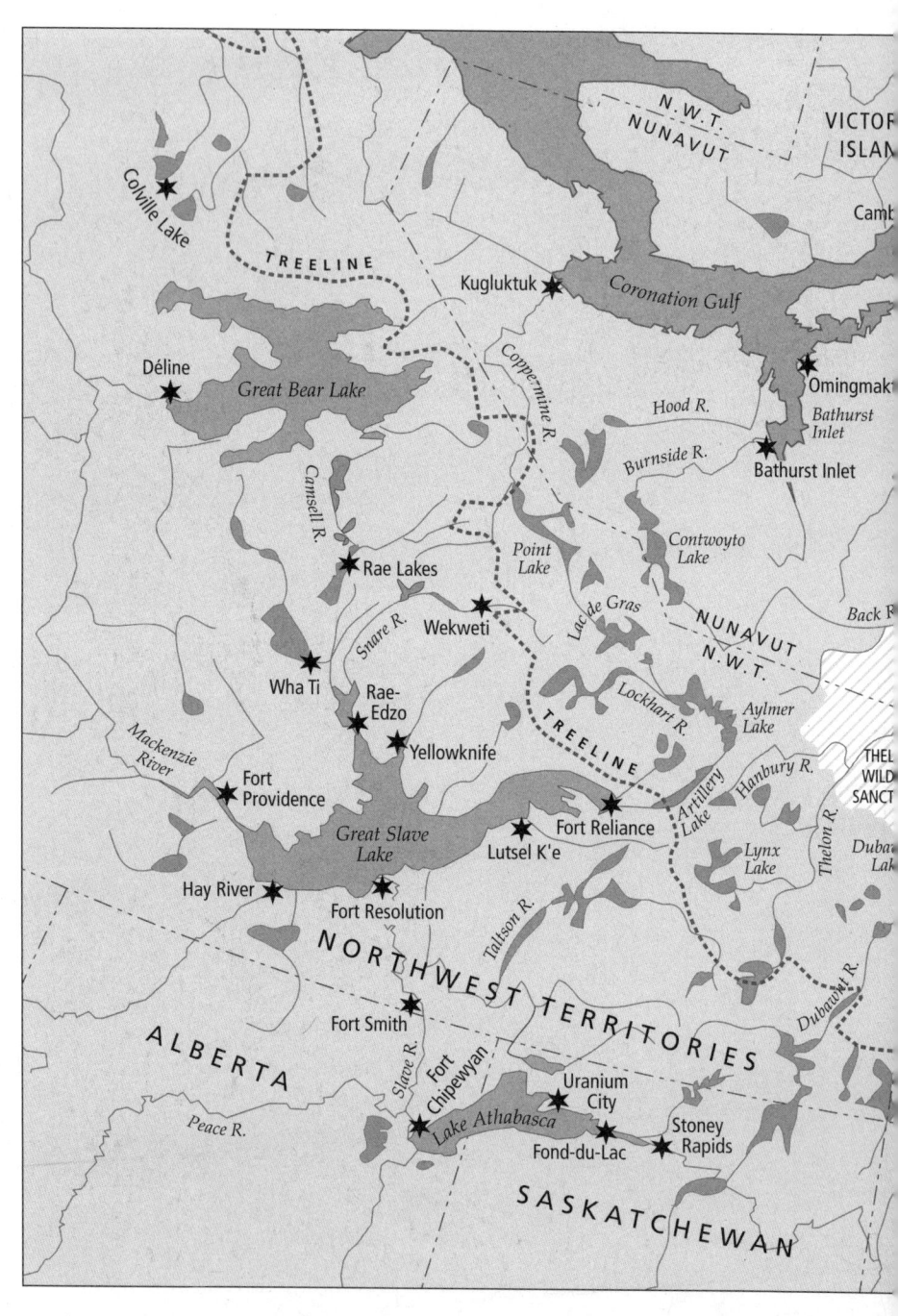

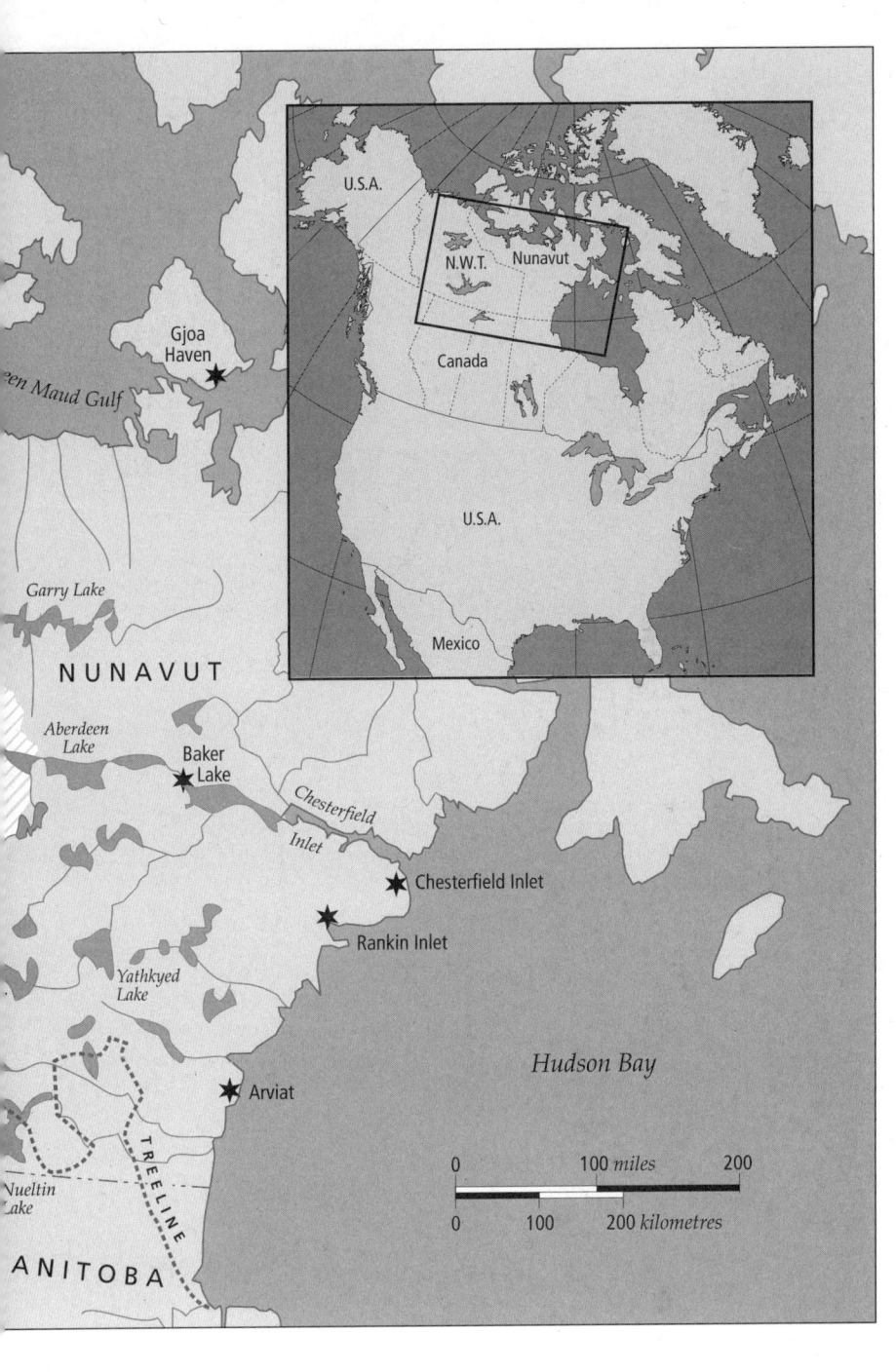

Discovering Eden

A LIFETIME OF PADDLING ARCTIC RIVERS

Alex M. Hall

KEY PORTER BOOKS

Copyright © 2003 Alex M. Hall

All rights reserved. No part of this work covered by the copyrights hereon may be reproduced or used in any form or by any means—graphic, electronic or mechanical, including photocopying, recording, taping or information storage and retrieval systems—without the prior written permission of the publisher, or in the case of photocopying or other reprographic copying, a license from the Canadian Copyright Licensing Agency.

National Library of Canada Cataloguing in Publication

Hall, Alex, 1942-
    Discovering eden : a lifetime paddling arctic rivers / Alex Hall.

Includes bibliographical references and index.
ISBN 1-55263-221-0

    1. Hall, Alex, 1942-   2. Canoes and canoeing—Northwest Territories—Fort Smith Region. 3. Canoes and canoeing—Nunavut—Keewatin Region.   4. Fort Smith Region (N.W.T.)— Description and travel.   5. Keewatin Region (Nunavut)—Description and travel. I. Title.
GV776.15.N57H34 2003   797.1'22'097193   C2003-902608-6

The publisher gratefully acknowledges the support of the Canada Council for the Arts and the Ontario Arts Council for its publishing program.

We acknowledge the financial support of the Government of Canada through the Book Publishing Industry Development Program (BPIDP) for our publishing activities.

This book is printed on acid-free paper that is ancient forest friendly (100% post-consumer recycled paper).

Key Porter Books Limited
70 The Esplanade
Toronto, Ontario
Canada M5E 1R2

www.keyporter.com

Design: Peter Maher
Electronic formatting: Jean Peters

Printed and bound in Canada

03 04 05 06 07 5 4 3 2 1

For my father,
Malcolm MacLean Rose ("Mac") Hall (1903–1970)
and my mother,
Mildred Isabel Hall, née MacLennan (1913–),
who instilled in me a love for wild things
and wild places

Contents

Foreword / 13
Acknowledgments / 15
Preface / 19

Part I: Early Years

The Journey / 23
Where Wild Rivers Run / 32
Alone on the Barrens / 45

Part II: Canoe Arctic, Inc.

Getting Ready / 53
Canoe Trips and People Dynamics / 55
Tough / 60
On Paddling a Canoe / 64
A Close Call / 70
Lost / 71
Bushed / 72
A Dangerous Swim / 74

The Storm / 75
The Big Wind / 80
Respect / 81
Larry's Inuit Graves / 83

Part III: The Wildlife

The Ways of the Caribou / 87
Guardians of the Gates / 90
White Wolves of the Tundra / 95
The Big Black Ox / 105
Encounters with Grizzlies / 107
Ravenous / 115
Power over Grizzlies / 117
The Elusive Wolverine / 120
Treed / 122
My Bear Alarm / 124
Underfoot / 126
Winter Journey on the Barrens / 127

Part IV: Memorable Characters

A Most Remarkable Client / 131
Jack / 132
Billy / 133
Mandy / 136
The Last White Trappers / 139
John Hornby: Myth and Reality / 144

Part V: Family Connections

Impressing Lia / 149
Graham's Beach / 151
More Bear Stories / 152

Part VI: Some Favourite Places

The Most Beautiful River / 157
Thelon River / 158
The Place of Power / 164
The Oasis by Canoe / 165

Part VII: Changes

Wildlife and Land Use / 175
The Battle for the Thelon / 188
On the Brink / 192
The Vision / 204

Epilogue / 217
Index / 219

Foreword

Nine of us, new to each other, stood in a loose circle on the tundra, totally diminished by a big, big land. This was it. The legendary "sermon." Our guide, Alex Hall, was about to establish the ground rules for our canoe trip through the Barren Lands of Canada's Central Arctic.

I can't remember every detail, though they're all recorded in a tattered little notebook that Al keeps in his hip pocket for handy reference. What I do recall, clearly, was Al himself pointing out that our "fun and enjoyment" was definitely a *third* priority! First came safety, second came respecting the environment. Without the first two, there would be no fun or enjoyment.

Having been a guide myself, I was especially interested in Al's approach. Even his more quirky requirements (always tip the wet end of an unloaded pack towards the sun to dry and never leave it sitting on sand) proved to be the best way to do things. Not surprising really. Thirty years of experience is bound to teach you something useful, especially when you've been the *only* full-time guide in that particular part of the country.

What followed for all of us that summer were two weeks of heaven on earth: huge skies, fresh fish, aboriginal artifacts, grizzlies, wolves, moose, caribou, muskox, eagles, peregrines, gyrfalcons, tundra wildflowers, crystal clear waters, and Al's signature dish—

warm bannock before dinner to restore tired muscles at day's end.

Every day, the nearest road was hundreds of miles distant in any direction, unless you count the ribbons of ancient caribou trails tracking the eskers. Knowing there is still this much true wilderness on earth leaves a person permanently changed. Perhaps it's the result of having been touched by what the Dene call "The place where God began."

Eden indeed, but truly beyond description. The Barren Lands are felt in your bones, not conveyed in sentences. You have to step out of a tent for that expansive view and first lungful of fresh morning air, or feel your canoe run with a strong icy current, or maybe just look up at a raven while brushing your teeth in the evening.

The power of the Barren Lands may be beyond words, but you won't come any closer than those on the following pages by Alex Hall. They flow from both practical knowledge and a loving eye, from knowing every gravel bar on a river, to wanting your ashes scattered over one in particular. Perhaps most important, Al's words carry with them an ember to rekindle hope for all of us in the modern conservation movement. Our hope and determination, in alliance with the Dene and the Inuit, is that Canada's magnificent Central Barrens will remain a big wild piece of our planet, championed and cherished by the people who live there.

MONTE HUMMEL
President
World Wildlife Fund
Canada
February 2003

Acknowledgments

I had always hoped I would write a very personal book like this one some day, but I expected that day would come a little later in life. In truth, writing this book proved to be a lot of fun, because nearly all of it flowed from my memories and the stories I tell my clients.

My friends Kevin and Rita Antoniak, Jay and Carolyn Pritchett, David Pelly and Monte Hummel, as well as my sisters Helen Griffiths and Jane Bousfield, reviewed the original manuscript and suggested helpful ways to improve it. My friend Cormack Gates critically reviewed "Wildlife and Land Use" (Part VII), as did Anne Gunn, caribou biologist for the Department of Resources, Wildlife and Economic Development (RWED) in Yellowknife, NWT. Anne also provided me with current estimates of caribou populations and maps of the calving grounds of the Beverly, Bathurst and Ahiak caribou herds. George Bihun, Conservation Officer in Stoney Rapids, Saskatchewan, and my friend Adrian D'hont of RWED in Yellowknife supplied me with data on the numbers of wolves killed by trappers in the Northwest Territories. Vicky Johnston of the Canadian Wildlife Service in Yellowknife enlightened me on various aspects of the Queen Maud Gulf Migratory Bird Sanctuary. A number of friends and clients have graciously contributed photographs for the book. In writing "The Vision" (Part VII), I made use of ideas, observations and even some wording provided by Monte Hummel and David Pelly. I am indebted to all of these people for their generous contributions to this book.

A few parts of this book have been published previously. "Where Wild Rivers Run" (Part I) originally appeared under the title "Seven Rivers North" in *The Beaver* (Summer 1976). "Alone on the Barrens" (Part I) was also first published in *The Beaver* (Spring 1980). Parts of "White Wolves of the Tundra" (Part III) were taken from "Encounters with the Tundra Wolf" (*The Beaver*, Winter 1976) and "Wolf Watching on the Tundra" (*Up Here*, July/August 1988). The epilogue and part of the preface first appeared as an essay entitled "What the Barren Lands Mean To Me" in *Heron Dance* (No. 21, 1998).

I am indebted to my friend Sherry Pettigrew, who volunteered her time and professional services to help me in a number of ways. Most important, Sherry provided me with valuable advice on prospective publishers and on the technical aspects of preparing my manuscript. I don't know how I would have coped without my friend and next-door neighbour, Steve Malcolm, who expertly transformed my handwritten manuscript and edits into type on his computer. I thank Anna Porter, publisher of Key Porter Books, for her faith in my original manuscript. Thank you, Michael Mouland and Doris Cowan, my wonderful editors, who made a real difference to this book, particularly in the earlier sections.

I am grateful to my clients of the past three decades (most of them Americans), whose patronage has permitted me to live my unique lifestyle. My thanks also go out to the many bush pilots who have flown my parties safely and efficiently into and out of the Barren Lands over the years, especially Dave Van Ember, Alan Loutitt, the late Billy Bourque, Ian Ross, Terry Best and Doug Williamson.

Thank you Lia, my wife and partner in life for fifteen years; thank you for helping me overcome my terrible shyness and find the courage to fight for the things I believe in. And finally, I want to express my gratitude to Monte Hummel—a kindred spirit—for his unwavering enthusiasm for this book throughout its evolution, for his faith in my ability to write it, and for using his considerable influence and resources to ensure this book found an appropriate publisher.

Preface

For the past three decades I have spent my summers canoeing the gin-clear rivers of the Barren Lands and adjacent forests in the Northwest Territories and Nunavut. For most of those years I have made my living as a canoeing guide. In writing this book I have drawn upon my best and worst experiences—especially the latter because it's the things that go wrong that make for the most interesting stories. Above all, I have tried to convey what the Barren Lands mean to me, and why the word that always comes first to my mind—the only word that is adequate—is Eden.

How can I explain the lure of the Barren Lands? What is it that makes them such a magical place, such a powerful place?

I always think of their physical beauty: the green, rolling, tundra hills; the clarity of the air; the vivid blues of the lakes and rivers; the sand beaches; the eskers (always the eskers); carpets of wildflowers; the crimson fall colours; the glorious, sun-drenched, arid summers; the enormous skies; the wind, the wind that is your best friend when it blows away the blackflies and your worst enemy when you are immobilized by its fury. I think of the animals, the wildness of the place and, perhaps most of all, the feel of the size and scale of the wilderness. But this country is much greater than the sum of its parts.

The Barren Lands are a gigantic triangle of roadless tundra west of Hudson Bay. Twice the size of either Texas or Alberta, they form the largest wilderness left in North America. Although the word *tundra* may conjure up an image of a desolate, treeless plain, this mainland portion of the Canadian Arctic is vibrant with life. Here lie the breeding grounds of countless birds, including millions of geese, and the ranges of some of the world's last great migratory herds of large herbivores and the predators that follow them. With almost half of its surface covered by water, this vast tract of tundra is perhaps best visualized as a lake-strewn northern prairie, but a prairie with more rugged hills than flatlands, and pockets of spruce trees that go on for a hundred miles or more beyond the so-called treeline. Boulders and rock outcrops of the Precambrian Shield litter this land and serpentine, sandy eskers course over it. For a few months of summer, it is greened by a carpet of dwarf shrubs, lichens, mosses, grasses and sedges.

Europeans explored parts of this immense piece of Canada's North as early as the 1700s, but most of it remained unknown to white man until the twentieth century. Little of it was mapped before the 1960s. Hundreds of rivers and hundreds of thousands of lakes are still unnamed. The first Europeans to set foot in this region called it the Barren Grounds for its general absence of trees. The name stuck, as did Barren Lands and Barrens, the modern names of choice.

For thousands of years, nomadic aboriginal hunters roamed across the Barren Lands in pursuit of caribou herds that once numbered in the millions. But now, their descendants—the Dene and Inuit—have moved to permanent settlements scattered around the edges of these treeless hills and plains. The huge interior of the Barren Lands is almost empty of people today.

The Barren Lands belong to the caribou. Myriads of their trails are carved into the surface of the land everywhere you go. Their great migrations are, without question, the most awesome wildlife spectacle in North America today. I've often stood on a hilltop where I could look out five or ten miles in all directions and see nothing but a flowing mass of caribou stretching to the horizons. Sometimes, they have kept moving by like that for an entire day, hundreds of thousands of animals in a single herd. You have to see something like that to really believe that it is still possible. The first time you do has to be one of the great moments in your life.

A variety of birds and large mammals still inhabit the Barren Lands in impressive numbers. If they didn't, this place would be little more than a wearisome wasteland. On one recent canoe trip of nineteen days we saw somewhere between 50,000 and 100,000 caribou, 237 muskoxen, thirty-one wolves, three wolverines and two grizzlies. It was a zoo! In my diaries I've recorded every large mammal I've encountered in thirty summers of canoeing in the Barren Lands. I've seen millions of caribou, thousands of muskoxen, hundreds of moose and over a thousand wolves and a hundred grizzlies. I've had many thrilling experiences with arctic wildlife, but most of my favourites have been with the tundra wolf, an animal of mystic intelligence.

When I try to think of negative aspects of the Barren Lands I can think of only one—the bugs. As my clients in July often remark: "This place would be a paradise if it wasn't for the bugs." To which I always reply: "Yes, but if it wasn't for the bugs there would be people all over the place." The blackflies are like the tsetse flies of Africa; they keep the people out.

I've travelled around the world and in many parts of North America, but for me there is no place else on earth that rivals the beauty of the Barren Lands. To be sure, there are some monotonous and forbidding parts, but in the central Barrens, at least, those are not the easiest parts to get to. And along the river systems, there are places that take your breath away—real Edens that you almost resent canoeing through because as you pass you are leaving them behind. You think all winter about going back to those places. It seems that the more you see of the Barren Lands the more you have to return. You can never get enough. A hundred lifetimes wouldn't be enough.

But there's a lot more than beauty or animals in my obsession with this land. A place can be beautiful, but if it isn't wild it can never be exciting. With close to a half million roadless square miles, the Barren Lands are the most exciting place left on this earth, as big and wild and remote as you can get. Except for the transcontinental jets passing high overhead, there are almost no signs of man's passage. Most of this pristine land looks and feels much the way it must have centuries, even millennia ago.

In this collection of stories, essays and commentaries about the land, its animals and the lessons they have taught me, about my experiences in that remote wilderness and my hopes and dreams for its future, I have written about things that are as important to me as life itself. If this book teaches others to value the Barren Lands as I do, it will have accomplished its purpose.

PART I

Early Years

The Journey

In August of 1958, Dr. Douglas Pimlott was invited to Camp Ahmek, a boys' camp in Ontario's Algonquin Park, to talk about the research he was conducting on wolves in the surrounding area. His talk ended with a wolf howl, a research tool that he had pioneered. I was a fifteen-year-old camper at Ahmek at the time, and Pimlott's visit made a lasting impression on me. Our paths would cross again in 1966, and the rest of my life would be shaped by it.

For as long as I can remember, I have been fascinated by wild animals. As a boy, I had as pets practically every wild bird and mammal that could be found near my southern Ontario home. My captured companions included various small birds, crows, owls, rabbits, squirrels, foxes and raccoons. I think it's fair to say that until I was in my twenties I thought of little else but hunting, fishing and wild animals.

With my two younger sisters, Helen and Jane, I was raised in my father's ancestral home in Brampton, a small town with agricultural roots, close to Toronto. My father was a professor of radiology at the University of Toronto and had a large medical practice, with offices near the university. My mother, who was from Cape Breton Island, had been a registered nurse in Toronto when she met my father at the beginning of the Second World War.

There's a legend in my father's family that suggests that my lifelong obsession with wild things may have come to me quite naturally. Although our family name is Hall, the story goes that the Hall line is actually descended from a union some two hundred years back between an aboriginal woman and a Hudson's Bay Company explorer by the name of MacLean. My great-grandmother Hall was also a MacLean, so it's intriguing that my grandfather and then my father were both marked at birth by the ancient, but by then quite rare, MacLean clan trait of six fingers on each hand.

Our home in Brampton was a tiny farm of sorts. We had a good-sized barn and five acres of pasture on a river valley where massive elm and black walnut trees grew. We kept a small flock of Suffolk sheep, an old racehorse for my sisters to ride, a retired farmer's team of Clydesdales and an assortment of chickens, bantams, pheasants and mallard ducks, most of which ran wild.

My father was really a farmer at heart. On days off from his medical practice he ran a small beef cattle operation that eventually grew to seventy-five head of registered Herefords on two hundred acres near Orangeville. He also had large plantations of Christmas trees and red pine near Sundridge, Ontario. Once, he even grew pussy willows and sold them commercially. My father loved hunting and fishing and spent a lot of his time in those pursuits, usually with me at his side. He was a keen bird watcher and was considered a naturalist and a conservationist of note in his day.

By the time I was six or seven my daily chores included looking after our flock of sheep, feeding the chickens and collecting the eggs. On weekends there was often work to do on the farm near Orangeville. Nevertheless, I always had plenty of free time.

Our river valley in Brampton had its fair share of fish and wildlife, but just five minutes away by bicycle lay wide open farming country.

Until I left home for university at seventeen, I spent most days hunting some species of wildlife, usually on the farms just outside of town. I don't remember how old I was when I started hunting on a regular basis with a .22-calibre rifle, but I had a 20-gauge shotgun by the age of ten. It all seems rather frightening by today's standards, but my father instructed me in the safe handling of firearms at a very early age. He trusted me and I never let him down.

When I turned sixteen, a newly acquired driver's licence and my father's pickup truck allowed me to pursue wildlife much further afield. From feral pigeons, crows, pheasants and ducks to groundhogs, rabbits, hares and foxes, I hunted almost every kind of small game in the area. Duck hunting and speckled trout fishing were two of my father's greatest loves. He introduced me to both when I was four or five years old, and duck hunting soon became my greatest passion. With our ever-present Chesapeake retriever, my father and I hunted ducks together at least once a week every fall until he died in 1970.

I spent every summer of my boyhood in the rolling bush country of the Canadian Shield, a few hundred miles north of Toronto. For the month of July we were always at our summer cottage on Lake Bernard near Sundridge. However, my father was never one to sit on the beach. Every morning we either pruned Christmas trees on our plantations or bushwhacked in to one of our trout-fishing streams, dragging our bamboo poles behind us.

Since my father and I caught more trout than anyone else in the area, we went to considerable lengths to keep our fishing spots secret. We parked our truck—always a green truck—in a place that was well hidden by trees, and we even brushed out our tire tracks where we drove off the dirt roads. My father also had a small fishing shack on a lake near the boundary of Algonquin Park. About once a week we'd walk in there and spend the night. It was there that I first heard wolves howling. My father woke me one night when I was about seven to listen to them.

For eight or nine Augusts in the 1950s, my parents sent me off to Camp Ahmek in Algonquin Park. Ahmek had a strong program in canoeing instruction and canoe tripping. Although my family kept an old Peterborough canoe at our cottage, it wasn't until I had spent many summers at Ahmek that I became a proficient canoeist.

At university, I was younger than most of my peers, and it showed. Most of them were busy planning their careers and their lives. I didn't have the slightest interest in doing either.

As ever, hunting continued to be the main focus of my life. A friend of my father's owned coonhounds, and I had been spending more time hunting with him with each passing year. At the age of eighteen, I acquired an outstanding young Redbone hound and became a dedicated coon hunter. This took up a lot of time at night, when I should have been studying. On fall weekends, when many of my classmates were drunk or chasing women, I was back home in Brampton hunting—day and night.

My parents hoped I would become the family's fourth-generation medical doctor, but I had no interest in medicine at all. When I graduated in 1964 at the age of twenty-one, with a degree in biology and history, I still had no idea what I wanted to do with my life. I decided to take a year and travel around the world. I hoped I could find myself. When my grandmother in Cape Breton died, she had left me the grand sum of $3,500. I went around the world in fifty weeks on that opportune inheritance.

Back in Canada, I decided to pursue a graduate degree in biology, specializing in animal ecology. In those days ecology was a word that very few had ever heard. That's when I met up with Doug Pimlott again.

By now, Doug was a well-known environmentalist and wolf biologist at the University of Toronto. He took me on as a master's student. My grades were good, but Doug later told me that it was the independence and maturity I had demonstrated in circling the globe on my own that had been the deciding factor. In the summer of 1966, I worked on wolves in Algonquin Park with Ed Addison and Dennis Voigt, both of whom became lifelong friends. This gave me the chance to brush up on my canoe tripping skills, which had lain dormant since Camp Ahmek days. The next summer, I began my master's research on beaver and wolves in Algonquin Park and near Georgian Bay.

At the time, Doug had students studying wolves and caribou on Baffin Island in the Canadian Arctic. In 1970, when several of us were finishing our theses, Doug asked us to go to Baffin for the summer to work on some of his wolf and caribou projects. Ironically, in view of my later career, I was the only one who *wasn't* interested in going. The other students' photographs of Baffin didn't make the place look very inviting, and I wasn't sure I could afford the time: I had a thesis to finish. And there was another factor: the recent, sudden death of my father had left me in a state of shock. However, in the end I decided to go because the trip was free and I thought I might never get another chance to see the Arctic.

That decision, which seemed of little importance at the time, changed my life forever. I expected the Arctic to be rather sterile and monotonous, but it turned out to be the most exciting place I'd ever been. And I had seen a good chunk of the world.

I'll never forget the first time I looked down on the tundra wilderness from our chartered airplane over west-central Baffin. Since our departure from Frobisher Bay (now Iqaluit) we had been flying above low clouds; then, as we descended, the tundra suddenly appeared about three hundred feet below us. There were snow geese and caribou down there on lush, green tundra.

This was real wilderness, the stuff my dreams were made of. The hair stood up on the back of my neck, and my imagination flew. I was hooked—instantly hooked! The southern Canadian wild places were mere child's play by comparison. I would never be the same again. At that moment, though I wasn't really aware of it yet, the course of my life veered off in a radically new direction.

When I graduated with my master's degree in the spring of 1971, all I wanted to do was spend the summer on the tundra again. I even turned down a job studying furbearers for the Mackenzie Valley Pipeline Project in order to do it. But how exactly could I manage it? I was a canoeist. I wanted to be able to really cover some ground. Virtually the only way to travel around Baffin Island was on foot.

The answer was the mainland tundra, with its lakes and rivers galore. My father had subscribed to *The Beaver*, the Hudson's Bay Company magazine, which focused on northern life and history. In it, I had read an article by someone who had canoed down the Thelon River in the Barren Lands. That was where I wanted to go.

In July 1971 my friend Ron Thorpe and I drove to Yellowknife, then flew out on a float plane to begin a thirty-seven-day canoe trip down the Hanbury and Thelon rivers to Baker Lake. Recreational canoeing in the Barren Lands was in its infancy then. We were only the eleventh party to canoe the Thelon River for pleasure.

The tundra of the upper Hanbury River was almost identical to west-central Baffin Island, but the scale of the Barren Lands made Baffin seem small by comparison. And the Thelon was completely unlike anything I'd seen in the north: the valley's extraordinary beauty and its rich wildlife made a deep impression on me.

However, at that point, I had no idea that I'd ever return to the

Barren Lands. I knew it was time to settle down to my chosen career as a wildlife biologist.

The only trouble was, I couldn't find the kind of job I wanted. And I looked all over Canada. As a stopgap I compromised, taking a job in Ottawa as an environmental consultant. I hated it. I loathed the nine-to-five mentality. I felt imprisoned by it. After spending the summer of 1972 at my desk in Ottawa, I vowed I would never spend another summer in a city or in southern Ontario again.

While I was slaving away I often thought of the Barren Lands. One of the things that had impressed me about our trip on the Thelon was how much easier it was than I thought it would be. That got me thinking. I reasoned that even though the Thelon was one of the most remote places in the world, the canoe travel there wasn't especially challenging. Just about anybody could do a trip like that— and I could take them there. The light bulb went on, and almost overnight I found myself planning what I hoped I would do for the rest of my life: operate guided canoe trips in the Barren Lands. The Thelon River would be a great place to start. As it turned out, a lot of people around the world were having similar ideas in the early 1970s. As a result, the adventure travel industry was born.

The next summer, Dennis Voigt and I spent eleven weeks traversing the mainland Northwest Territories by canoe, from the Saskatchewan border to Coppermine (now Kugluktuk) on the Arctic coast, a distance of almost twelve hundred miles on four different river systems, mostly in the Barrens. It was, and remains, the greatest single adventure of my life.

At that time, about the only tourism businesses in the Northwest Territories were a few hunting and fishing camps and lodges. At the end of our canoe trip, Dennis and I met with the government officials in charge of economic development and tourism in

Yellowknife. They clearly thought I was extremely naive to imagine I could make a success out of the kind of business I was proposing. They agreed to give me a licence to try it, but they weren't encouraging. In the words of one of them, I was fifteen or twenty years ahead of my time.

To be honest, I think most of my family and friends agreed with those officials in Yellowknife. But I felt compelled to follow my dream. I knew if I didn't, I would probably look back in old age and wonder "what if?" Besides, I was confident I could make this business work. I decided I would give it five years. If the clientele I expected failed to materialize in that time, it wouldn't be too late for me to return to my original profession as a wildlife biologist.

By the fall of 1974 I had established Canoe Arctic, Inc. and was busy launching my career as the first professional canoeing guide in the Northwest Territories. Business, however, failed to take off: I had just one client in 1975 and one again in 1976. Those were the toughest years of my life. But I am a very stubborn man, and I still believed my dream would come true. I kept the faith and I kept on advertising.

During the summers of 1974 through 1976 I went on lengthy, exploratory canoe trips—usually alone. My travels took me from the forested regions north of Saskatchewan as far as Baker Lake near Hudson Bay and Bathurst Inlet on the Arctic Ocean. I started in late May and finished up in mid-September. I paddled rivers that had never been paddled before. (Some of them remain my secret to this day.) My eight-week solo journey in 1975 was the toughest canoe trip of my life; I portaged literally hundreds of miles.

My patience paid off. In 1977 business suddenly boomed and by 1979 my canoe trips were 100-percent booked. The spectre of a desk job as a biologist was dispelled; I would never look back. I decided to move permanently to Fort Smith in the Northwest Territories. I liked the town and its surroundings, and throughout the late 1970s, it had been my main base of operations. I'd work out of Fort Smith for the first four weeks of the season, drive up to Yellowknife for six more weeks of trips, then return to Fort Smith for another four to six weeks. By 1979, mineral exploration north of Great Slave Lake was becoming so intense that there was no longer any advantage for me to operate out of Yellowknife, and in any case I could afford a house in Fort Smith (I couldn't in Yellowknife). Today, I continue to operate Canoe Arctic, Inc. as a one-man business based in Fort Smith.

In 1981 Lia Ruttan, a young social worker from Seattle, joined one of my trips. With roots in Minnesota and plenty of canoe tripping experience, Lia had long dreamed of canoeing the Barrens. When she returned the next summer we fell in love, then married in 1984; in Fort Smith, Lia taught and supervised the social work program at the Territorial College located in town. With most of her summers free, she was able to assist me on my canoe trips until our first son, Graham, was born in 1990. Our second son, Evan, was born in 1992. Sadly, our marriage ended in 1998.

Over the decades, my guiding service has allowed me to meet a lot of wonderful people, including many Americans. Some of my clients have become my friends, returning summer after summer. The worst day of every year is always the day I finish my season in September. If anything, my love for the Barren Lands has grown stronger with the passage of the years. To my mind, I have the best job in the world and I intend to keep doing it as long as I'm physically able.

Where Wild Rivers Run

On June 4, 1973, Dennis Voigt and I stood on the shore of an unnamed lake and watched our chartered float plane lift off the water, then disappear into low clouds scudding in from the north. We were alone on the Saskatchewan–Northwest Territories border some fifty miles above Lake Athabasca. Over the next seventy-seven days we would paddle our canoe north out of the forest, then across the Barren Lands to the community of Coppermine (now Kugluktuk) on the Arctic Coast. Most of our 1,150-mile route lay along seven rivers: the Dubawnt, Ethen-eldili, Thelon, Mary Frances, Hanbury, Lockhart and Coppermine.

Our preparations during the previous winter had included a review of both historical and modern accounts of travel on the Lockhart and Coppermine rivers. Famous among these is Sir John Franklin's narrative of his expedition down the Coppermine in 1821. In the historical sense, only two small sections of the initial five hundred miles of our route had been roads of discovery. J.W. Tyrrell had ascended the upper Thelon River to the mouth of the Ethen-eldili River in 1900 and Guy Blanchet had explored the upper Dubawnt River in 1926. However, we found their descriptions almost entirely lacking in navigational information. And we could not turn to the aboriginal people; they no longer had the knowledge. Except for a few trappers south of treeline during the winter, most of the region we intended to travel through had been uninhabited for generations.

So it was with a sense that we were facing the unknown that we set out, trying to deduce what we could from the maps. We were completely dependent upon our own resources, with no means of communication should a serious accident occur along the way. We hoped that by descending the upper Dubawnt and Ethen-eldili rivers early in the season, when water volumes are usually high, we would have an easy and speedy passage down their gradients. There was a great deal of country to be covered, and we knew from the outset that we had to average a hundred miles a week if we were to reach our destination before the brief arctic summer ended. Apart from the Coppermine River, our route up the Lockhart and Mary Frances rivers and across the big lakes was not geared for speed. We could be windbound for days or immobilized by lake ice any time before mid-July. The warmth of an early northern spring, however, did much to allay our fears.

We began with a forty-mile push through a maze of small lakes to catch the headwaters of the Dubawnt River flowing northeast into the Barrens. Going was slow: our seventeen-foot aluminum canoe was loaded down with food and equipment, and everything had to be transported over the many portages in three heavy loads. Pleasant park-like country compensated for the hard work. The lakes were clear and the surrounding low, sandy hills supported well-spaced spruce trees growing over a thick carpet of lichen. A profuse network of trails woven over the landscape showed that this was prime winter range for barren-ground caribou. Wolf scats bristling with the hair of these northern deer were scattered along the trails, and sometimes we found the bleached bones of the prey, or an occasional display of massive antlers still attached to a skull.

When we entered the Dubawnt River we were confronted with a magnificent sandy esker that had shaken off the forest except for a few perfectly formed spruce trees sprinkled along its heights. The valley was comparatively lush; thickets of willow, dwarf birch and alder were a more common sight and the river was interspersed with small marshes. Mallards and pintails flushed along the river edges; mergansers, a few scaup and large flocks of scoters scuttered across the pools below fast water; then, in a widening, we stopped to watch four bald eagles fishing over some rocky shoals. We made our first camp at the head of Ivanhoe Lake, where the Dubawnt plunges over a great rock, forming twin waterfalls. Soon we were catching northern pike of up to twenty pounds on almost every cast.

Downstream, the Dubawnt forms good-sized lakes, but to negotiate the river sections between these lakes required a combination of portaging, wading and dragging the canoe down shallow riffles with some welcome stretches of paddling and navigable rapids. Once, when the river split into two branches, we managed only nine miles in a full day's travel. Each lake, however, was a pleasant interlude that offered a variety of open, windswept campsites free from the swarms of mosquitoes that had emerged during the recent succession of warm, sunny days. There was little evidence of human occupation, except for a couple of crumbling log cabins perched high above the river, showing that trappers had once been active in the area.

After eighty miles on the Dubawnt, we struck a more northerly course towards the treeline, by way of an exquisite chain of lakes whose shores glistened with sandy beaches and interlacing eskers. Barren hilltops began to poke up through the thinning forest, and numerous peat meadows ended on the lakeshores in steep, slumping banks. I remember days of strong southerly winds whisking us over the lakes before great, rolling waves; the endless sun; portaging above the forest along the top of an esker; the last small bands of geese hurrying north; and between lakes, shallow rocky creeks alive with grayling.

At one in the morning on June 19, in the brief twilight that passes for night at that latitude, we paddled out onto Big Esker Lake and pitched camp for a few hours' sleep on the edge of the Barrens. In the sunlight later that morning we could see the abrupt line of forest just to the south, then the small clumps of stunted black spruce that marched away to the north, hugging the great runs of sand beaches along the lake. Beyond the shoreline a vast, treeless plain rolled away in the distance giving a sense of tremendous space.

The source waters of the Ethen-eldili River, Big Esker and White Wolf lakes had great expanses of cold water that disappeared into the horizon with no land in sight. As luck would have it, we crossed them both on a flat calm, but the heat was oppressive and great clouds of blackflies followed us out from shore for miles on end. Part of the monotony of crossing these lakes was relieved by watching for lake trout. They seemed to be breaking the surface for insects everywhere. At one point we noticed what appeared to be smoke from a campfire swirling up from a small island about a half-mile ahead. As we drew closer, we heard a high-pitched whine, then fifty yards away we saw that the "smoke" was actually millions of flying gnats.

From White Wolf Lake the Ethen-eldili River winds through a system of small lakes flanked by hilly barrens, then finally plunges over a short series of steep rapids into the Thelon River. Although no rapids were marked on our maps of the Ethen-eldili, we encountered them by the dozens. All except three were navigable, but many were shallow—which could prove troublesome to canoe travel by midsummer. One section near the river's confluence with the Thelon sported an exhilarating mile-long torrent; it took all the strength and skill we could muster to keep our canoe on a safe course away from the rocks.

The eskers along Ethen-eldili River valley were long and sinuous with sweeps of clean white sand, blanketed here and there by a smooth greenery of heath plants. The spruce trees that grew along the heights were tall and symmetrical, and the sand dunes often cradled little round lakes of dazzling blue or emerald green. Clumps of smaller spruce and an occasional lofty tamarack provided sanctuary for a few typical forest dwellers such as robins and red squirrels.

As we descended the Ethen-eldili, tundra forms of wildlife made their first appearance. Scoters gave way to old squaw ducks; there were jaegers, willow ptarmigan, red-throated loons, arctic ground squirrels and grizzly bears—their tracks, anyway. The trodden-down country along the Ethen-eldili showed that caribou in incredible numbers had passed this way on their northern migration some six weeks before.

The Ethen-eldili also seemed to be the summer retreat of thousands of non-breeding Canada geese. Being flightless at that time of year, they would slink ashore as we approached, then, with their long necks stretched close to the ground, they would run off with an awkward gait that caused their up-tilted tails to wag to and fro in the most comical manner. One of their favourite tricks was to dash overland to cut off a bend in the river so that they could re-enter the water far ahead of us. Sometimes they just disappeared inland. Being curious, we once tracked a flock of one hundred for a mile and a half over sand dunes. We gave up when we finally saw a lone goose topping a distant hill, still going like a racehorse.

When we entered the Thelon, just forty-five miles from its source, we found a wide, fast-moving river flowing between high gravel banks. Although the landscape was rather flat, and less interesting than that of the Ethen-eldili, it was pure pleasure to coast along at speeds up to ten miles per hour with no rapids to negotiate. Our second day on the Thelon was highlighted by the surprising sighting of a large bull moose, a full seventy-five miles from the forest.

In reaching the Thelon by way of the Ethen-eldili River, we had travelled a virtually unknown route leading into the heart of the Barrens. To the west of the Ethen-eldili are several other water routes leading to the Thelon, including one described by Blanchet as the road used by Dene muskox hunters in the late nineteenth century. The Dubawnt and Kazan rivers, the better-known southern approaches to the tundra and its interior, were explored by the Tyrrell brothers in 1893 and 1894.

On June 29 we left the Thelon and easily tracked and paddled our canoe three miles up the unbelievably clear waters of the Mary Frances River. Travelling a river by canoe can be likened to driving along a highway in a car. Scene after scene rolls by, but one feels somewhat apart from the land. So as often as we could, we hiked off to explore. In the beautiful wide, sandy valley of the Mary Frances, we set out on foot from our campsite and soon came face to face with two white wolves. We stood still, men and animals, observing each other quietly. After a while one of the wolves trotted off. The other, a large male, retreated only a hundred yards or so, then began to howl and bark. Assuming we had stumbled into the vicinity of a wolf den, we soon located a likely-looking sandy hummock about a half-mile away. Sure enough, there we found some shallow, interconnecting tunnels containing two dun-coloured pups about three weeks old. Under the watchful eye of the big white male we removed these two shy little bundles of fur from the den for a few photographs, then returned them. The adults seemed unperturbed. About an hour later we observed one of them stretched out asleep beside one of the entrances to the den.

A study conducted by Ernie Kuyt for the Canadian Wildlife Service in the 1960s showed that wolves seldom raise large litters of young in this part of the Barrens, because caribou are temporarily out of reach to the north during much of the denning period. Lesser beasts can only offer these large predators a marginal living. Southward-drifting caribou would not likely return to the Mary Frances country until after mid-July. Then later in August, the pups would be old enough to take up the nomadic way of life with their parents.

Upriver from our camp, the Mary Frances made a big bend to the south as it fell steeply over the lip of the Thelon valley. It was here that J.W. Tyrrell was thwarted in his attempt to chart a water route west to the Lockhart River in 1900. Sending his men downstream to return to the Lockhart via the Hanbury River, Tyrrell walked overland, to rejoin his party on Artillery Lake. With the advantage of modern maps we elected to bypass this section of the Mary Frances by making a seven-mile portage north of the river. Since we still had to transport everything in three loads, the distance we actually walked was a punishing thirty-five miles.

In two days we rejoined the Mary Frances in country completely lacking in the sandy hills and stands of spruce that had characterized the Thelon just a few miles below us. From this point, our course lay across a number of lakes of varied size. Buoyed up by the good weather, the complete absence of ice and our progress to date, we were now confident that we could easily reach our destination of Coppermine by September 1. Then, on Mary Frances Lake, we were pinned down in the lee of an esker for forty-eight hours by thunderstorms and gale-force winds. Incredibly, this was the only time during the entire summer that weather conditions prevented us from travelling.

We finally sighted caribou as we neared the Hanbury River on July 9. A tight formation of five hundred bulls streamed down a distant hillside, turned at a small lake, and headed our way. Minutes later the herd was racing alongside us under a weaving tangle of over-sized antlers. Stragglers passed us throughout the remainder of the day, all of them being driven upwind by the insect horde. Although the blackflies were numerous, we did not find them voracious; but they were driving the caribou frantic. When the poor beasts tried to stop to graze, the flies would close in, causing the animals to shake or buck, then go charging off again. Caribou are easily approachable, and we often attracted distant animals by waving a white handkerchief. While some showed an obvious curiosity in our presence, many simply ignored us, having no apparent fear or knowledge of man.

Even that night, there were still a few caribou passing through our camp to cross an adjacent narrows on Smart Lake. By midnight, when Dennis and I were in our sleeping bags writing up some notes, we heard a wolf howling some distance away. In response to our imitations of its cry, the animal soon appeared at the narrows, then splashed through the shallow waters and walked into our camp. A few yards away from our Egyptian cotton tent it stopped to examine its surroundings in the fading light, taking no particular notice of the peculiar white object with two human heads poking out through the flap. It then retraced its steps and sauntered along the far side of the narrows, stopping every few yards to utter a lonesome call. Earlier that day we had seen another wolf standing on top of a downed bull caribou floating in water about fifty yards from shore. On this day, July 9, the Barrens came to life for us. The open terrestrial sea had been empty; now a new dimension had been added.

The next day we found the scattered ruins of several mineral exploration camps that had been active in the upper Hanbury area during the late 1960s. At one of these camps we gathered up a big bundle of unused claim stakes. They were a precious find in a land where the only firewood came from a few pencil-thin bushes of dwarf birch.

On July 11 we entered the Lockhart River at the south end of Clinton-Colden Lake. This was the great crossroads of the Barren

Lands. It was difficult to escape the sense of history in that lonely place, for the land must still look as it did when the early explorers first saw it. Samuel Hearne passed this way in 1771 on his overland trek from Hudson Bay to the mouth of the Coppermine River. Sir George Back had come through here in 1834, bound for the river that now bears his name; both Hanbury and Tyrrell had passed by at the turn of the nineteenth century en route to the mysterious Thelon. Yellowknife and Chipewyan Dene, and fox trappers in the 1920s, had all regularly come this way.

Upriver, the Lockhart formed four great lakes with stretches of fast water between them. Our luck held as we pushed on, encountering gentle breezes on the lakes and strong tail winds on a few of the river sections. The Lockhart tumbled down considerable grades in places, but we usually found favourable conditions along the edges for tracking our canoe upstream, keeping portaging to a minimum. West of Aylmer Lake the country became more rugged. Although the hills were littered with boulders, the lowlands were lush with green meadows and extensive growths of dwarf birch. A few stunted spruce trees reappeared and willows up to ten feet in height grew in some favourable locations along the river.

In the late afternoon of July 24 we were making our way over a string of small lakes leading into the Coppermine River when we began to see a few small bands of caribou travelling high along the distant ridges. Their numbers quickly increased, and we soon realized these must be the forerunners of one of the world's last great wildlife spectacles. By evening, caribou were flooding into the area—fifty here, a hundred there, herds of three hundred, five hundred, a thousand—as far as the eye could see there were caribou, all moving unhurriedly southwest towards treeline. After supper we went out and walked among the herds. The pace was leisurely; for the hot weather had done its work well. Blackflies and mosquitoes had virtually disappeared during the second week of July. Now the caribou had time to fatten up on grasses and sedges and browse among the thickets of dwarf birch.

They were an odd-looking crew. The bulls, although scarce, looked noble enough, but the cows were a bare-bones lot, still shedding their coats of ragged winter hair. Calves were there by the hundreds—cream-coloured, cinnamon and chocolate brown—chunky and full of play. We watched them splash into the water behind their mothers and gamely swim the lake. It was hard to believe that most of them were only six weeks old. They had done a lot of travelling between here and the calving grounds east of Bathurst Inlet, over 250 miles away. Moving en masse, the cows were calling out continually to their wayward calves: a mounting swell of grunting, guttural sound announced the arrival of each new wave of animals that swept into sight.

When we awoke the next morning, caribou were still pouring in from the north. Travelling only seven or eight miles that day, we passed thousands, all of them moving slowly in the same direction. Several times we eased our canoe within twenty-five yards of herds that were feeding and resting on shore. That afternoon we came upon a large concentration of animals filing across a narrow lake in two long columns. Standing in the chest-high dwarf birch that grew along the edge of the lake, we watched hundreds swim ashore and stream by us, almost within touching distance.

For over a hundred miles down the Coppermine, caribou were never long out of sight. Groups of twenty to a hundred seemed to occupy every lush little valley tucked away among the eighty miles of rugged highlands along Point Lake. On more than one night we were awakened by herds passing within a few feet of our tent. Confronted with these overwhelming numbers, one can understand why some northerners believe that millions of caribou still roam the Barren Lands. However, we had also passed through hundreds of miles of tundra to the southeast that were almost lifeless. For a full 175 miles along the Lockhart River we had seen only four caribou.

On August 3 we re-entered the forest north of Point Lake after nearly seven hundred miles of travel on the Barrens. Here we met two groups of fly-in fishermen, the only people we encountered on our route. By then we had run out of tobacco and were smoking the year-old leaves of the bearberry plant. We had developed a strong craving for sweets and fresh fruit. We were as gleeful as small children when our hosts treated us to lavish meals, then presented us with a generous supply of chocolate bars and enough tobacco to see us through the rest of the trip.

With fast river currents and only three short portages ahead, the remaining 275 miles of our route required little more than a week's travel. After a brief passage through the forest, the Coppermine re-emerges onto the tundra, but scattered white spruce trees grow along its valley floor for another 150 miles. As we continued downstream, the valley deepened. More and more, the spruce were restricted to the lower flanks of rugged hills that towered a thousand to fifteen hundred feet above the river. Now that we were within striking distance of our destination, with plenty of time to spare, we relaxed and spent many long days climbing into hidden valleys along cold, gushing streams and roaming the hills high above treeline. Caribou were scarce now, but we often saw moose, which had moved into the bottomlands in recent years. Golden eagles swept the open gravel ridges hunting for ground squirrels, and down on the river there were tundra swans, some late broods of widgeons, and great flocks of pintails and mallards. Although the fishing was usually disappointing, one

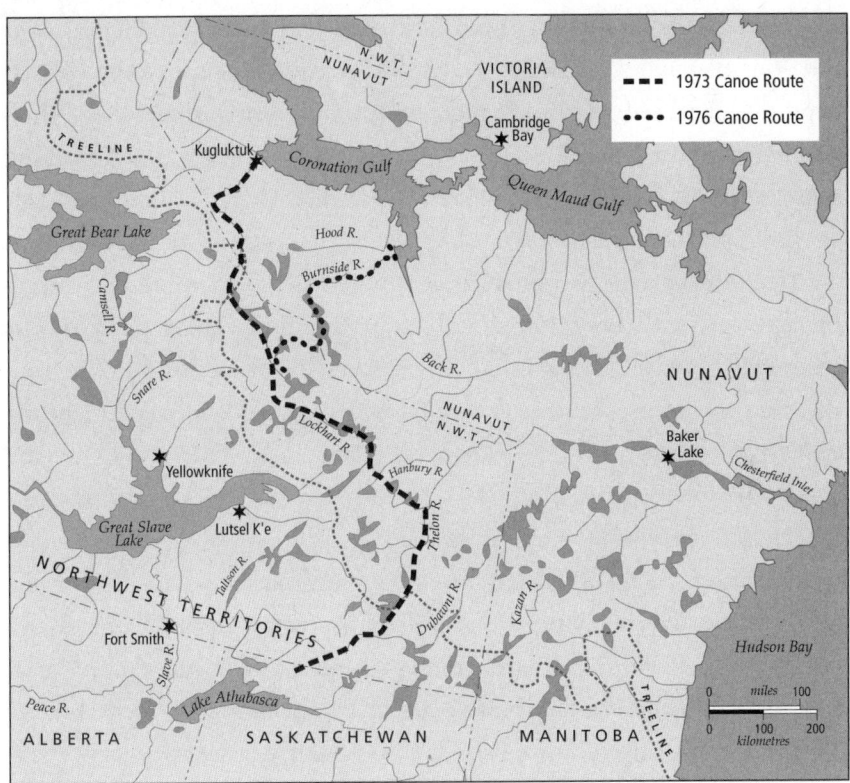

evening we caught some big pink-bellied arctic char, about three feet in length.

In mid-August the weather turned cold and wet with intermittent snow showers and heavy frosts at night. Decked out in nylon rain suits and inflatable life vests, we set out from Muskox Rapids on August 19. The river was now bitterly cold and clouded by the murky, rain-swollen waters of the Kendall River. Below us, the Coppermine was a continuous succession of rapids as it fell five hundred feet over a fifty-mile run to the sea. Twisting through deepening canyons of red sandstone and white clay cliffs, the river channel was frequently whitened by rows of huge standing waves that often smashed over the gunwales of our canoe. The wildest section was a six-mile stretch beginning with Sandstone Rapids, where the river dropped more than twenty-five feet per mile. By staying on the inside turns we avoided most of the turbulence, but on two occasions we had to head gingerly for shore with several inches of water in the bottom of the canoe.

The next morning we arrived at Bloody Falls, so named by Samuel Hearne to mark the massacre of a small Copper Inuit party by his Chipewyan Dene guides in 1771. Schools of arctic char, fresh from the sea, were running up the river, so we stayed for several hours casting our lures at these leaping silver fish. The banks of the remaining eleven miles of the Coppermine were dotted with Inuit tents, and alongside each were the red fillets of char drying on wooden racks. The river was now slow and easily navigable for the motorboats full of waving and shouting Inuit that zipped by us, heading upriver towards Bloody Falls. A cold drizzle was falling that afternoon of August 20, when we paddled out onto the Arctic Ocean and pulled into the community of Coppermine, ending what we will probably remember as the greatest experience of our lives.

Two days later, aboard a DC-3, we flew up the Coppermine valley, bound for Yellowknife. The land we had crept across in weeks of travel we now whisked over in a few minutes. Down there we had been insignificant, powerless in an ocean of hills that rolled away to every horizon, seemingly forever. Now, from the aircraft, the land no longer seemed limitless, no longer remote for mechanized man. Life in the Barren Lands has undergone great changes, and aboriginal peoples no longer roam across the vast interior regions, but the face of the land is still unaltered, still unscarred by the destructive uses of modern technology. Yet because of the advances in that technology this land is vulnerable as never before.

Alone on the Barrens

It was June 21, 1976, and I was flying out to the Coppermine River. In the two years since the trip I went on with Dennis I had become an experienced barrenland traveller. This time, I would be exploring alone.

As the little Cessna float plane droned on, I peered down to watch a huge ice-filled lake inch slowly by below. My plan called for the pilot to put me down on the river at Lac de Gras. From there I would paddle my sixteen-foot fibreglass canoe downriver to Lake Providence, then ascend an unnamed river rising sixty miles to the northeast, cover eighty miles across Contwoyto Lake, then follow the precipitous Burnside River 165 miles to Bathurst Inlet on the Arctic coast. The Burnside was a river I had long wanted to attempt. My friend Jay Pritchett had descended the Burnside the previous summer, and his party was probably the first ever to do so. His enthusiasm for this river had inspired me to paddle it.

Now I was flying over the big, ice-choked lakes that formed the headwaters of the Lockhart River just north of the treeline. Spring had come early south of Great Slave Lake, where I had spent the past three weeks, but here in the western Barrens the breakup was not particularly far advanced. I had arrived a week too early, but I had planned well and was confident of success. Even if ice conditions delayed me by two weeks I had seven weeks' supply of food to see me through to my destination.

The pilot eased the Cessna into a widening of the Coppermine, just below the solid white expanse of Lac de Gras, and a few minutes later I was standing on shore watching the aircraft roar off to the south again. I was alone in this vast, uninhabited wilderness.

Summer was ripening south of treeline, but here it was only

beginning. The dying remains of a few snowdrifts were still in evidence along the rugged, rocky hills, and the tundra reflected a brownish tint, not yet fully greened by the almost endless sun. Caribou were far off to the northeast, but the land was pulsing with birdlife ranging from little Lapland longspurs to terns, jaegers, ducks and loons.

The first obstacle in my path was nine miles of rotten candle ice filling the basin of Desteffany Lake. At first my way appeared to be effectively blocked, but then I discovered the southwest wind had pushed the ice fifty yards off the southern shore of the lake, allowing me to pass. The rivers flushing into the southern end of Lake Providence had cleared out enough ice by June 25 to give me access to the unnamed river that I would ascend through Yamba Lake and beyond. Now began the hard work of wading up rapids and transporting four loads of food and equipment over each portage. Along one series of rapids I found some canoe-patching material—two rolls of birchbark that had probably been dropped by some party of Dene in the nineteenth century. It was possible that I was the first canoeist to pass this way since those times.

When I reached Yamba Lake I climbed up on a high esker and used my binoculars to search for a passage through the ice. The lake sprawled out in all directions. Only fifteen miles separated my position from a little bay where I would resume my course up the river, but the only water visible led out along a big island towards the middle of the lake. Through a combination of fantastic luck and a good deal of skidding my canoe over ice, I managed to cross the lake that day by following a series of leads along a chain of islands.

Northeast of Yamba Lake the rugged, stony hills give way to a smooth, green, gently rolling country characteristic of the great plateau that cradles Contwoyto Lake at an elevation of 1,460 feet. I was almost looking forward to my confrontation with this great lake as an escape from the desolation I was crossing. The birdlife that had been so abundant along the Coppermine had shunned this land, and had it not been for the occasional bugling of the old squaw ducks the entire country would have seemed empty of life.

When I arrived at the main body of Contwoyto Lake, all that could be seen was a great, white, shimmering plain of ice that disappeared into the horizon. A little open water allowed me to cross to the island, where a lonely radio station had been built to assist aircraft in crossing the Barrens. I would have to wait for the ice to open up a channel. The three men who operated the station were most hospitable and gave me the freedom of their quarters throughout my stay. A few hundred yards away stood a handful of crude wooden shacks that had been the homes of the last Inuit to inhabit the inland regions of the continental Barrens. They left for Coppermine in 1974 and did not return.

At the radio station I was giving serious consideration to turning south for Great Slave Lake. It seemed impossible that a canoe could advance very far in that ice within the next week or two. On the other hand, I had seen the miracles that the wind could perform, so I decided to wait. The very next day, on July 9, a southwest wind began opening up the western shore of the lake. I set out, and by noon I had advanced fourteen miles; then the water ran out. The next morning a west wind came up and I was off again, following the narrow passage along the shore, paddling twenty-two miles this time. I couldn't believe my good fortune as I made camp that night. Only twenty-five miles of shoreline travel separated me from the outlet of the Burnside River.

Everything seemed to be going my way. Willow and dwarf birch suitable for firewood were exceedingly scarce in this country but in this location wood was no problem. Like the campsite Dennis and I had used on the Hanbury, this was a spot that had been intensively prospected in the early 1960s after a gold strike, and claim stakes and scrap lumber lined the beach. Just to the north, the beautiful Peacock and Willingham Hills loomed up, promising more interesting terrain. And the land was coming to life. Flocks of ptarmigan occupied the few thickets of dwarf birch and hundreds of long-tailed jaegers lined the edge of the ice. Later that evening a big white wolf sauntered through camp. I felt I had reached a turning point.

The next day it became evident I had indeed reached a turning point, but not the kind I had anticipated. A northeast wind began to move the ice in, and the weather turned bitterly cold. I was trapped there for three days, watching the water freezing between the pans of candle ice, locking me in even tighter than before. When the shore ice began to shift on the fourth day, I decided on a course of action. From a vantage point on a hill I had seen some open water far out on the lake that I believed would lead to an ice-free shoreline along the far side. I hastily constructed a sled from the abandoned lumber on the beach, loaded it aboard my canoe, then paddled out towards the middle of the lake through a jigsaw puzzle of broken ice.

About a mile out I came to the edge of solid ice. I loaded my canoe and packs on the sled to begin hauling them towards open water about two miles away. But the sledding proved more laborious than I had expected, and the sharp porous ice quickly cut the wooden runners to ribbons. Changing my tactics, I began to portage everything over the great white expanse in short stages. Several times I came to newly frozen leads, but I was able to break through in the canoe and float everything across. When the far edge of the ice field could no longer support my weight, I pushed the loaded canoe over the surface until I reached open water. This water led me in a circuitous route to the far side of the lake, where I was relieved to find an ice-free corridor along the shore. I was roundly congratulating myself on my ingenious accomplishments of that day when a freshening south wind began moving the ice in, stranding me again before I could advance a single mile up the lake.

When the wind stopped two days later, I set out again with a new plan of attack. A good deal of backtracking and portaging allowed me to recross the lake so that by mid-afternoon I was advancing in open water past the location where I had earlier abandoned my sled. An unfavourable north wind was building, but I managed to clear two critical points of land scant minutes before the ice pack came crashing ashore. Jubilant, I pitched camp late that evening beneath the Peacock Hills near the outlet of the Burnside River. I had finally escaped my prison of ice.

When Samuel Hearne and his Chipewyan guides reached the Burnside in 1771, they met some Yellowknife Dene hunting caribou at a traditional summer crossing not far below Contwoyto Lake. Dene have not hunted caribou here for well over a hundred years, but occasionally pilots report enormous herds passing through this area en route from the calving grounds at Bathurst Inlet. I hoped to be lucky enough to encounter this remarkable summer migration.

On July 17 I set off down the Burnside with the feeling that I was embarking on a great adventure. The maps showed that most of this stretch of the river dropped between eleven and twenty-two feet per mile—a statistic that on the Canadian Shield generally indicates dangerous rapids and much portaging. Around noon I came to Belanger Rapids, where Sir John Franklin's party had crossed in 1821 on their gruesome death march to treeline. Just below these rapids I noticed that the rocks on the hills were moving. Caribou! A massive column of caribou was swarming down the hillsides two miles away. I swung the canoe in the heavy current and scrambled up on top of a nearby knoll, where I could see more of the surrounding area. An incredible tide of living flesh was surging towards me, fanning out as it approached. It parted and flowed around me. There were tens of thousands of caribou. The cows and their young calves were grunting and honking, but the steady din of these guttural sounds was so muffled by the wind that the great herd seemed to be passing in almost ghostlike silence. After five hours the last of the column had gone by and the land lay empty again. A biologist I later met who had flown over this herd several days before had estimated its numbers at 125,000.

My next week or so on the Burnside was almost idyllic. On the days I chose to travel, the river sped me along for twenty-five or thirty-five miles. The Burnside was full of rapids, but the drops were evenly graded so that most of them were easy to negotiate and made for delightful canoeing. The long, sunny days turned hot, and even the swimming became pleasant. As I continued downstream, the valley grew lush with grasses and clumps of willow and alder. Big, soft, green hills billowed up seven hundred feet or more above the swirling river and against them, like little black ants, I sometimes saw muskoxen grazing. There were small bands of caribou, some young wolves at a den, surprising numbers of ground squirrels and birds of many kinds.

One day I came upon a big bull muskox giving himself a dust bath near the top of a fifty-foot embankment along the river. I had beached my canoe and was changing the film in my camera when the muskox suddenly charged down the bank towards me. I had had unpleasant encounters with these monsters before, so I lost little time in leaping back into the canoe. Unfortunately, my hasty departure was delayed when the canoe became lodged on some rocks.

Meanwhile, the beast had pulled up short of the canoe and was rooting up the ground with his horns, thoroughly spraying me with dirt in the process. As I made frantic efforts to free the canoe and escape, a number of loose film canisters rolled off a packsack and fell into the river. My fear turned to anger and, scooping the precious film out of the water, I rather impolitely told the brute where I wished he would go. With an amazed look on his face, he suddenly turned tail and galloped away. Only then did I realize that until I shouted at him he had probably not noticed I was there.

As I approached the coast, the hills grew much steeper and rockier and lost much of their richness and charm. The river rushed between wide boulder beds and cut along towering banks of sand and clay, where I sometimes heard a falcon cry or glimpsed a golden eagle as it took flight. Above its delta, the Burnside squeezes between the narrow rock walls of a spectacular canyon that funnels its churning waters down four miles of chutes and falls before dumping it into the sea. Other than a ten-yard liftover below Belanger Rapids, this was the first portage I had had to make since embarking on the river. Although I was able to shorten this portage somewhat by paddling through part of the canyon above and below Burnside Falls, the day's work was made miserable by the oppressive heat and the swarms of blackflies that had suddenly emerged.

On July 27 I paddled down the last few miles of the Burnside to Bathurst Inlet. For the next few days I wandered along this surprisingly lush coastline; the highlight was my walk to the Hood River, where Wilberforce Falls drops 165 feet into an awesome gorge with sheer rock walls two hundred feet high. The timing of my arrival at the falls proved perfect, for there I found my friends Jay and Carolyn Pritchett, who had just led their party on the first-ever descent of the Hood River.

A few days later we all converged on Bathurst Inlet Lodge to await our chartered float planes from Yellowknife. Bathurst Inlet was seething with the activity of over one hundred prospectors and their supporting aircraft. At the lodge, Jay and I discussed how only a few years earlier we could travel for hundreds of miles across this land without encountering any sign of modern man. Now the camps and helicopters deployed in the quest for minerals were hard to avoid. We were witnessing an acceleration in man's exploitation of the Barren Lands, a phase that would eventually shrink the vastness of this last great wilderness.

My travels in the early and mid-1970s laid the foundations for my professional guiding career. I had learned a great deal about the country and how to live and travel in it safely and efficiently. In just five years I had become an old hand.

Beginning in 1977, guiding canoe trips became my full-time occupation. I continued to travel many of the rivers that Dennis and a few of my other partners and I had explored in the early years, but it wasn't long before the blitz in mineral exploration on the western tundra limited my activities to more eastern regions. With the quality of wilderness waning quickly on the Coppermine, I conducted a few final commercial canoe trips down this once great river in the late 1970s. Further east, the ever-pristine Thelon River was firmly established as the backbone of my operations. Pioneering canoe routes on rivers that have never been paddled before is something I still do occasionally, but for the most part in the company of my clients. By 1977, my grand adventures into the unknown were essentially over.

PART II

Canoe Arctic, Inc.

Getting Ready

"What do you do all winter?" is a question I'm often asked. People think that a seasonal business as small and as simple as mine, with no more than fifty-four clients a year, must practically run itself—that like the bears, I must sleep all winter and rouse myself just in time for my first clients as they step off the plane in June. The short answer is that in this business you spend all winter getting ready for summer. By the time the canoe trips begin, the real work has already been done, and the enjoyable part begins.

In September, after the last of my clients have departed, I try to think of my business as little as possible. September is my time off, when I do the things I've loved doing since I was six or seven years of age. This often puts me into a canoe again. After three months of back-to-back canoe trips and mothering nine clients per trip, I'm usually bone-weary by September. Although I love the suppleness of my body by the end of the summer, I know I won't begin to feel stronger until I regain some weight.

September is also the month when I must plan my next year's advertising campaign and start writing those big cheques to American magazines that display my advertisements. Up to 40 percent of my annual clientele is repeat business, but I don't make a nickel on that first 40 percent. The only thing that keeps my business viable year after year is spending large sums of money on advertising. In my line of work, if you don't market your business successfully, you won't have a business. It's as simple as that.

By the time the snow flies in late October, I've obtained a quote on the air charter rates for the following summer and I'm updating my trip descriptions, revising my brochure and solidifying my plans for canoe trips over the next two years. I inventory my equipment, repair anything I consider worth the effort, and order any necessary replacements. Some of this gear is custom-made and can take up to a year for delivery. As a result, I'm usually stockpiling major pieces of equipment a year or two before I'll need them. I also keep a lifetime supply of some items on hand. For example, I own close to two hundred Duluth packsacks and eighty or ninety pots of various sizes, every one with bails for carrying them.

I have correspondence to deal with every day, answering letters and mailing out brochures. Nowadays, there's also e-mail to answer. By nature, I'm well organized and I pay attention to detail; over the years, I've developed hundreds of pages of lists so that all of those details are at my fingertips.

Winter is also the time when I take my annual courses in first aid and CPR, go over numerous small details with my clients for each of the upcoming trips, and finalize my air charter reservations. For years I pored over sheaves of maps of canoe routes, but I hardly ever look at a map any more. By now, I've been just about everywhere I've ever been interested in going and I've examined almost everywhere else in between from the air.

Since making a living as a canoeing guide depends on my physical well-being, it's important that I stay reasonably fit. I do sixty push-ups and sit-ups every morning and walk three miles a day, regardless of the temperature. On some of the milder days I ski two or three times that distance. Until three years ago I ran on a regular basis.

In early April I order the bulk of my food for the summer and spend a good part of that month organizing and packing it. By May, most of the snow has melted and summer is no more than three or four weeks away. The rush is now on to have everything in place for my first trip in June. With the beginning of warm temperatures, I complete the last of my outdoor chores of varnishing paddles, rigging and seam-sealing new tents and doing some maintenance on my canoes. When my first clients step off the plane I'm as ready for them as I was a year before, almost to the day.

So even the quiet months are busy. Winter is when I get ready for the crazy season, the time of the year when my life shifts into high gear. In fact, there isn't a single month in the year that isn't part of the never-ending cycle: when I'm not in the Barren Lands, I'm preparing to go back there, back to the place where life is imbued with a sense of freedom, and where the magic of the wilderness calls me.

Canoe Trips and People Dynamics

Sometimes, that magical connection with the wilderness isn't easy to achieve, and our best efforts encounter setbacks. Just about every wilderness canoeist has a story about a group of friends who went on a canoe trip and came back hating each other.

Long periods in isolation have a way of magnifying the importance of little things that normally wouldn't bother you. Wilderness canoe trips also present situations that reveal the true character of the people you thought you knew.

I know of one group of six friends who started out on a month-long canoe trip in the Barren Lands, but aborted the trip after two weeks because they were constantly fighting. They couldn't agree about such simple things as when to travel, how far to paddle each day, when to get up in the morning and whether to run certain rapids or line or portage them. They had failed to agree on a few basic rules of conduct before they embarked on their trip, and they had no designated trip leader. They tried to reach all decisions on the spot, democratically, which unfortunately, is seldom a practical way to run a wilderness canoe trip. For the various party members to come together and operate as an effective team, there has to be a captain or benevolent dictator. Otherwise, chaos reigns.

The most extreme example of a canoe trip that got out of my control and went awry was certainly the one I took with Robert and his family.

Robert was a wealthy, self-made man who, in his youth in the 1930s, had been part of an extended canoe trip through northern Manitoba to Hudson Bay. It had been a wonderful experience for him, and when he discovered me in 1978 he thought he had found the right person to help him organize a similar kind of experience for his family.

At that time, I was still spending my winters in southern Ontario. Robert was planning a business trip to Toronto that winter, and he wanted to meet me to talk about his ideas for the canoe trip. He probably wanted to size me up, too. However, his planned trip to Toronto fell through, so he convinced me to visit him at his home in the southern United States for a long weekend, all expenses paid. That was my first mistake: I was already doing things on Robert's terms. But I'm sure Robert was used to getting his way.

Robert was very concerned about his family's comfort, and when he started itemizing the kinds of food he wanted on the trip I tried to tell him that with such elaborate menus we would be spending all our time cooking, eating and washing dishes instead of enjoying the unique things he wanted to show his family in the first place. But he wouldn't budge. That's when I made my second mistake. I should have had the courage to tell Robert he had to do it my way or find another guide. But I didn't.

In late August, I finally met all nine adult members of Robert's family. They arrived in Fort Smith aboard a specially chartered DC-3, because Robert wanted to reach and leave Fort Smith on Sundays, when there was no regular service. Then we had to add an extra aircraft to our fleet before we left Fort Smith, because some of Robert's family objected to having to sit on their packs. (It was common practice in those days to remove the seats on float planes to economize on space.)

It was obvious from the start that few of Robert's family members were interested in the trip. They rejected all of the standard rules about keeping their gear light or travelling efficiently. His wife wouldn't come out of her tent in the morning till water had been heated for her bath and brought to her. Robert's daughter, in particular, appeared to think her father had brought her to the most godforsaken place on earth. They were all incompetent paddlers, and they complained about everything. The only notable exception was Robert's oldest son. To make things worse, the weather was cold and wet.

At our campsites, Robert took charge. I was demoted to supplying the firewood. And they certainly burned a lot of wood. We usually ran two small cooking fires plus a gas stove, as well as a general warming fire. This was light years away from my normal no-trace camping practices. (I now must confess that I never led them to any of my good campsites along the route.)

The preparation of meals was so time-consuming that we never paddled more than three hours a day and most days for only an hour or two. It got so ridiculous that one day we packed up, got in our canoes, then made camp again less than a mile away. There were two rapids on our route where we had to line and wade the canoes. This normally results in my clients getting wet up to their buttocks. I had mentioned this at the planning stage, and since Robert wouldn't have his family getting wet he had purchased ten pairs of chest waders at a cost of one hundred dollars apiece. They filled up two packsacks. In the end, we only waded one rapid and the waders were used no more than five or ten minutes of the entire trip.

After eleven days of paddling we had gone a total of thirty-five miles on small lakes with one short portage. Normally, my parties require only two and a half days to cover this distance. However, it was important to Robert that we reach the end of our planned route, because I had told him about a trout-fishing paradise, a pool in the river where lake trout spawned around the first of September. At the rate we were going there was no chance we would get there, so Robert insisted I radio the air charter company in Fort Smith to request a move to the trout fishing hole. By some small miracle, I was able to contact Fort Smith on my HF radio the very first try. As usual, we could hear them clearly, but they had difficulty hearing us. Nevertheless, they understood our desire for a camp move and agreed to dispatch a Cessna 185 first thing the next morning. Then Robert told me that since I had Fort Smith on the radio I might as well order up ten T-bone steaks and three dozen bottles of wine! Fort

Smith deciphered the steak order all right, but understandably, they confused the three dozen bottles of wine for three. Robert was pretty disappointed.

Early the next morning, Scott arrived in a Cessna 185 and spent most of the day ferrying us down to a camp near trout paradise. As I recall, it required seven trips, forty miles each way.

In a Herculean effort the next day, everyone managed to paddle five miles to the fishing hole and, for once, the gods smiled upon us. It was a beautiful day and the fish were there by the truckload. In a couple of hours we caught and released well over one hundred lake trout. So I guess you could say that at least the trip ended on a high note. However, it had also cost Robert a small fortune in air charters to achieve it.

Of course, there were more issues at work here than the wrong person being in charge. The trip also failed because of inadequate experience in canoeing and camping on the part of the participants. Robert had dragged his family along on a trip that few of them were prepared for or even wanted to experience. Ultimately, the trip was doomed to failure because of the personalities, attitudes and inexperience of almost everyone involved.

Although I was greatly relieved when this nightmare ended, I felt sorry for Robert. He had wanted his family to feel something of what he had felt on that remote canoe trip in his youth so many years ago. And he'd gone to a lot of trouble and expense to try to accomplish that. In the end, we had all failed. But I, at least, had learned some valuable lessons that would serve me well in the future.

Ever since my experience with Robert, I have stuck to my first principle: as the organizer, guide and most knowledgeable person on the trip, I have to be the boss and run the trip my way. I make most of the major decisions and I never offer anything up for a vote where the consequences could jeopardize our safety or comfort. Of course, this approach only works well when it's unobtrusive and applied with a considerable amount of tact. A successful guide is a leader who can quickly earn the trust and confidence of his or her clients with a common-sense approach. To help prepare my clients for what lies ahead, I spend the first ninety minutes of every trip informing them about my philosophy of conducting canoe trips, the basic structure of each day, the dos and the don'ts, the safety rules, what my clients can expect of me and what I expect from each and every one of them. The rules are established from the very beginning.

Months before this information session, though, my clients have been thoroughly briefed about what to expect in the Barren Lands from the wild country itself.

Tough

The Barren Lands are tough country. The climate is one of extreme contrasts and there is almost no shelter. Winters are among the longest, coldest and darkest on earth. On the largest lakes, the ice can reach a thickness of eight feet and may not melt before August. Summers are short, but intense and often hot; the sun hardly sets. More water covers the surface of this land than almost anywhere else on the planet, yet technically, this is a cold desert with only eight inches of precipitation a year.

Even in July, the most hospitable month, it can snow. Temperatures can also soar to 100°F in July or drop 50°F within a twelve-hour period. Weeks often go by with hardly a cloud in the sky: summer means heat, relentless sun, plagues of biting insects, occasional rainstorms and strong winds that can turn frigid and reach gale-force levels. The elements, it seems, are hardly ever just right. But when they are, this iron land is transformed into an Eden. There's nowhere else more beautiful. There's nowhere else I'd rather be.

Someone once described the Barren Lands to me as young man's country. That may be so, but some of us who are far from young still spend our summers there. The Barrens will keep you young or kill you before your time. The Barren Lands will teach you more about yourself, and do it in less time, than anywhere else I know. If you want to find out the kind of stuff you're really made of, go on a long canoe trip on the tundra. If you're thinking of marrying, take your intended partner in life with you. I recommend it as a proving ground for any friendship, marital or otherwise.

When it comes down to only two people on a wilderness trip, compatibility is crucial. It works best when it's a true partnership. When Dennis Voigt and I were planning our eleven-week canoe trip across the Barren Lands in 1973, we agreed on one simple rule that, in retrospect, probably prevented a lot of strife. We agreed that the most cautious opinion would always prevail and that we would never argue about it. What this meant in practical terms was that if one of us, for example, favoured running a rapid, and the other wanted to portage, we made the portage without any further discussion.

Another beneficial practice we adhered to was to rest one day a week. This helped our bodies to repair themselves after days of strenuous travel. Canoeing the Barrens can be very hard work.

These days, my clients and I fly into the Barren Lands with our high-tech canoes and tents. We bring a satellite telephone and all the food we'll ever need sealed in plastic, foil and cans. We have gas stoves, Gore-Tex-lined rain gear and boots, bug-proof shirts and tents, headnets and DEET. Our life-support system weighs hundreds of pounds. It's as if we are visiting another planet. We need our canoes to carry it all. And it's still a severe test for many people.

You have to live and travel in the Barren Lands for at least a month or two before you can even begin to comprehend how tough the aboriginal people must have been to survive in this place. Every spring, with all of their possessions on their backs, they followed the caribou out of the boreal forest and across the Barren Lands for hundreds of miles. In a land where 40 percent of the surface is covered by water and with major rivers to cross, the travel was seldom easy. Women, infants, toddlers, perhaps even some of the old—they all made this journey on foot deep into the tundra and back again with no substantial shelter from the weather or insects. They were completely dependent upon stone-age weapons and tools for their food and what clothing and shelter they could manufacture along the way from caribou hides. Various nomadic aboriginal cultures succeeded one another over time, but the annual trek over the tundra in the wake of the caribou herds was sustained for eight thousand years. Today, it's almost impossible for us to appreciate how tough and resourceful those people must have been. We are mere butterflies by comparison.

Now we go to the Barren Lands on vacations, on canoe trips, for recreation. We fly in, in a matter of a few hours. But we are fragile. If we lost our life-support systems, most of us would soon perish. We are soft, but no matter, a month or more of canoe travel on the Barrens will whip almost anyone into reasonable shape. Most of us lose a pound a day for the first two or three weeks. I've seen some men drop forty pounds in a month. The Barren Lands make us lean and mean and turn our skin the colour and consistency of leather. We feel vigorous—alive. This is the way we were meant to live!

Physical toughness is an important attribute on any wilderness canoe trip, but mental toughness is of even greater value. There's much to be said for mind over matter. You're as tough as you think you are. You can do what you think you can. Unfortunately, most urban North Americans have no understanding of what their bodies are capable of. I've seen this over and over again on my canoe trips—big, strapping fellows who paddle like ninety-year-olds, who can't carry eighty-pound canoes and who favour thirty-pound packs. If you go to parts of Asia, you'll see skinny little people carrying loads that are larger and heavier than they are. Give that same load to the average two-hundred-pound North American male and he'll collapse in seconds.

My older clients have consistently proved much tougher and more capable than the younger ones. Each new generation seems to be softer than the one before it. A good case in point is Bob Hawkings, who was a frequent client of mine. In 1997, when Bob was seventy-eight, he brought his seventy-five-year-old friend Mary on one of my canoe trips. I put them together with a group of fifty-year-olds, who were concerned that Bob and Mary would slow them down. Bob had been canoeing his whole life, and I knew his physical capabilities were superior to most other people's, regardless of age. Sure enough, the fifty-year-olds were embarrassed to find they couldn't keep up with Bob and Mary.

When my father-in-law, Vern Ruttan, joined one of my canoe trips in 1987, he was well into his sixties. Vern was a university professor who was in reasonable physical condition, but he didn't do anything special to try to stay that way. He walked to the university every day and in the summer he canoed and fished a little in northern Minnesota, where he spent part of each summer. I teamed him up with James, a thirty-year-old New Yorker. I expected James's youth and strength to make the trip easier for Vern. As things turned out, though, Vern paddled stern throughout the trip and he carried their canoe most of the way over the portages, two of which were more than a mile. James couldn't portage the canoe very far, or at least he thought he couldn't. In the end, it was Vern who looked after James.

The difference, I realized, was that James had never lived anywhere but in New York City. He thought of himself as a jock because he ran, exercised and played sports, but he'd probably never done a day of physical work in his life. Vern grew up on a marginal farm in northern Michigan during the Depression. Vern knew what a day's work was, and in his sixties he still knew what his body was capable of. Mentally, Vern was much tougher than James.

As an example of what people are still capable of, I once guided a group made up mostly of women, who carried everything we had over a three-and-a-quarter-mile portage in a single day. Our canoes and supplies for the next two weeks required each of us to portage three heavy loads. We broke the portage into five legs and trudged back and forth for a total of sixteen miles each. At the end of that gruelling day, there was a real sense of pride in what we had accomplished. We achieved what we did because we believed we could.

On Paddling a Canoe

The canoe is the most practical, efficient and satisfying way to travel through wild country, particularly on the Canadian Shield, where a canoe will take you almost anywhere. It is silent, allowing you to stay in touch with the peaceful natural rhythms of wild places; you can quietly approach wild animals that are unaware of your presence. Canoe travel requires you to revert to the basics of life, where little else matters beyond food, shelter and the weather. And I know of no more enjoyable way to get yourself into top physical condition within a short period of time.

I've always liked to compare canoeing to skiing. To the uninitiated, both have the deceptive appearance of ease and simplicity. Both have a lot to do with balance. Anybody can step into a pair of skis for the first time and successfully glide down a gentle slope—just as anyone can hop into a canoe and cross a quiet pond or descend a smooth-flowing stream. But it takes many years of practice to become a good skier or a good canoeist.

Just as in skiing, you'll probably never become a great canoeist if you're self-taught. You'll pick up too many bad habits. Maybe I'm a slow learner, but during my boyhood I took lessons for about eight summers before I became a half-decent flat-water canoeist. It required some more years of practice before I became really good. Unlike the acquisition of my flat-water paddling skills, I had to learn white-water canoeing on my own while negotiating various rivers in the Northwest Territories. I learned that my flat-water skills served as an excellent base to expand from and that most of what constitutes white-water canoeing is learning to read the water and knowing what you can do with it—and what you can't. Instinctively, I developed the brace strokes well known to white-water kayakers and I do well enough, but without formal instruction it's unlikely I'll ever reach my potential.

Like every other eastern Canadian canoeist, I was taught the J-stroke, the correcting stroke that allows the paddler to keep the canoe going in a straight line without changing sides. However, when I was a budding young biologist in Algonquin Park, I developed what I thought was my own innovative version of this stroke. In my variation, the paddle in effect becomes a lever with the gunwale of the canoe acting as the fulcrum. My upper hand on the paddle grip stays below my nose and when the shaft of the paddle meets the gunwale my upper arm pries the power face of the paddle back and out. On the recovery phase of the stroke, the blade of the paddle knifes forward underwater and barely rises above the surface. When it does, it's feathered. When I use this stroke I paddle with my entire body. My arms barely move; they just rotate in their sockets. It's a very powerful and efficient stroke. It's also a very fast, short and choppy stroke. I usually paddle close to fifty strokes per minute.

More recently, I discovered this stroke has a name. It's called the Canadian stroke and sometimes the knifing-J or Northwoods stroke. It undoubtedly has aboriginal origins. It's a simple-looking stroke, but I'm told it's difficult to master. One of the disadvantages of this stroke is that it's very hard on paddles and gunwales. The shafts of my paddles wear out in two or three seasons and I have to reinforce the gunwales of my canoe where the paddle shaft strikes and rolls on them. Another disadvantage of the Canadian stroke is that after middle age sets in, the paddler is susceptible to tendonitis or tennis elbow from the repetitive snap of the upper arm. As a preventative measure I now wear tennis-elbow straps on both arms whenever I paddle any distance.

I'm an advocate of kneeling in a canoe, but the older I get the more I find I'm sitting. These days I kneel about 50 percent of the time when I'm sterning. When I'm soloing a canoe I can only paddle effectively in the kneeling position with the craft heeled over to one side. I've always been blessed with good knees, but these days I wouldn't last long without my knee pads.

Insufficient paddling skill is one of the most critical problems my clients must confront, with my help. Just as in skiing, canoeing is a lot more about technique than it is about strength. A little old lady who has paddled all her life will easily stay ahead of some big, strong fellow with limited canoeing experience.

Although I try to ascertain the paddling skills of my clients by having them answer a number of questions in writing, most people,

I find, greatly overestimate their abilities. A lot of people claim they know the J-stroke but turn out to practice what in the 1950s we called the goon-stroke. In this stroke, the power face of the paddle is turned in, not out as in the J. It's a very inefficient stroke because it puts a drag on the canoe and the rhythm of the stroke can never achieve any speed. (In a lifetime of canoeing I've only seen one person who could paddle effectively using the goon-stroke. He was a highly experienced Australian canoeist and he was as strong as an ox.) Most people using the goon-stroke manage to keep up with the J-strokers on a calm day, but when the wind blows they fall behind because the sternsmen do more steering than forward paddling. You only go as fast as your slowest canoe, so this can mean a lot of waiting on the part of the J-strokers.

Some inexperienced canoeists, far from doing too little, want to do way too much—they want to run dangerous rapids that are beyond their skill level. They may have difficulty trying to paddle across a windy lake in a straight line, yet they want to run challenging white-water before they have achieved acceptable flat-water skills. It's like trying to run before you can walk.

Sometimes, though, in safe conditions, I'll let people try things that I know will be hard for them. One lovely midsummer day on the Thelon a member of my group realized he'd forgotten his camera and binoculars at our lunch site, which we'd left about an hour before. Jim hailed my canoe and told me he wanted to go back for them. I knew that wouldn't be as easy as he thought, but I agreed that we'd make an early camp. Jim could take an empty canoe with three paddlers back to our lunch site.

This plan was approved by everyone, and just before three o'clock Jim and two volunteers set off to retrace our route back up the river to retrieve the camera and binoculars.

We were camped at the Gap, about ten miles below the Hanbury River junction. The Thelon is about as slow there as it ever gets. Nevertheless, the current is significant, and paddling against it is not easy. Back in 1899 and 1900, the first European and Euro-Canadian explorers managed it: they paddled quite quickly up the Thelon for hundreds of miles, and most of the river is a lot faster than where Jim was attempting to ascend it. However, men were made of sterner stuff back then. Jim and his crew had eight miles of the Thelon to ascend to reach our lunch site. I'm sure they thought they'd be back in camp in a couple of hours. I decided to let them find out for themselves.

After hours of paddling upriver, Jim realized they weren't making much progress. Though it would be a long walk, he decided the best plan was to leave the canoe and go on foot. All three of them walked up to the lunch site, where they had little difficulty in locating Jim's camera and binoculars, then returned to the canoe. They were three tired puppies when they paddled into camp later that evening. It was midnight, and they'd been gone nine hours!

Good equipment can help novice paddlers, but some special equipment, such as splash covers, is only for experts. It seems to me that for most canoeists, splash covers have more to do with appearances than practicalities. They'll never need them. They're like the nimrod cyclist in spandex shorts or the guy who packs a big gun in grizzly country. I've never canoed a river in my life where I needed a splash cover. Like any skilled canoeist, I can nearly always avoid big standing waves. Otherwise, I line or portage. In my opinion, splash covers should be left to the most highly skilled of white-water paddlers. Most canoeists shouldn't be out in the kind of water that requires a splash cover. In conditions that treacherous they're courting disaster.

I also have no use for synthetic or wide-blade paddles. Both are very recent innovations. I call them shovels because that's about how useful they are. I've tried them and I'll never understand what some people see in these awkward tools. I've always maintained that the quality of your paddle is more important than your canoe. As any proficient flat-water canoeist should know, you can't perform any kind of stroke very effectively or efficiently with a paddle blade that exceeds six inches in width. The usefulness of synthetic or wide-blade paddles is limited to white-water, especially shallow, rocky rapids.

The Indians and voyageurs used paddles that were only four or five inches in width. Mine aren't much wider. A lot of canoeists also use paddles that are much too short for them. When I'm standing, my paddle reaches my mouth—and I'm a tall man. I like heavy paddles, so mine are all made of solid white ash or sugar maple. (In spite of my biases, my wife made sure I purchased a good supply of light-weight, wide-bladed paddles for those of my clients who prefer them.)

Since the mid-1970s, canoeing has been my profession and way of life. For three or four months each year I spend almost every day in a canoe. This probably accounts for my rather utilitarian view of the craft. I see it primarily as a means of transportation or as a highly effective way of hunting ducks and moose. I never step into a canoe just for the pleasure of going paddling.

What I do like about paddling is that you are completely self-reliant. There is no dependence on mechanical devices. Canoe travel is utterly simple. You can load up your canoe with food and equipment, then paddle and portage a thousand miles across northern Canada without having to rely on anyone or anything else. For me, the canoe means complete freedom. It's the ultimate escape.

A Close Call

I've spent three or four months a year for thirty years canoeing the river systems of the Northwest Territories and Nunavut, mostly in the Barren Lands. In all those years, I've personally never had a scare or a close call on the water. I've only dumped or swamped a canoe once. That was back in 1976, and I don't plan on ever doing it again.

In all my years in business as a professional canoeing guide, I'm proud to say that none of my clients has ever had a serious accident or injury, on land or water. Over the course of a summer, we often run hundreds of rapids, but on average, my clients have upset less than one canoe per year. There are probably a number of reasons for our enviable safety record. The ones I would identify as being crucial would be my experience in assessing my clients' capabilities and my commitment to communicate clearly with them on how to avoid the potentially dangerous situations we encounter en route. Perhaps most important, I take charge of my clients and I never take chances.

Only once have I ever feared for the safety of my clients on the water. It was many years ago, late May or early June, on a river about a hundred miles south of treeline. The river was in flood. I had gathered my clients together to warn them that just around the next bend in the river was a major rapid that we'd have to line or portage. I told them to keep their canoes in single file and follow me, staying close to shore on the inside turn of the river. After we rounded the bend, we would come ashore using an eddy turn, then tie up to scout the rapid below.

All went according to plan until the last canoe. By then, the rest of us were safe on shore. When the last canoe came around the bend it was way out in the middle of the river. I shouted at the two men in the canoe to paddle like hell and get over to our side of the river. But the current was strong, and they didn't have the paddling skills required to make it to shore.

Just above the maw of the rapid was a small island, now submerged in the high water. All that remained of the island was a clump of white birch trees with the river racing through them. As the men in the last canoe were swept past us, I yelled to them to paddle into the flooded birch trees and hang on. This they managed to do. They were marooned about one hundred feet from us, but we strung some lining ropes together, threw one end out to them and hauled them ashore.

It was a very close call. They were very lucky that island was there. With the river in flood, the rapid below was a raging torrent. If those two men had been sucked into that rapid they could easily have been killed.

Lost

I've never been lost, but over the years at least four or five of my clients have been sufficiently confused that we had to go find them. In every case, this occurred south of treeline.

Once, when we were portaging along a raging cataract that could be heard for miles, one of my clients, who had been bringing up the rear, went missing. It turned out he'd wandered away from this thundering torrent at right angles. We finally found him some distance away. How anyone could get lost under these circumstances still mystifies me.

On another occasion, we were eating breakfast when I thought I heard someone calling faintly in the distance. I quickly did a head count and determined Mark was missing. When I asked Mark's wife where her husband was, she replied he'd gone off behind their tent to do his business before coming down to breakfast. However, Mark had apparently walked off in the wrong direction when he tried to return to his tent.

I found Mark almost a mile behind our camp. We were close to treeline and the trees were widely scattered. I spotted Mark several hundred yards ahead of me, dashing around aimlessly and yelling his lungs out. When I called back to him he evidently didn't hear me, but he failed to respond again when I was close to him. I finally walked up and put my hand on Mark's shoulder and called his name. His back was to me, and when I placed my hand on his shoulder he spun around. I'll never forget the panicky look in his eyes. He was completely out of control.

As a boy, I'd often heard stories about men getting lost in the bush and working themselves into such a frenzied state that they crossed roads without realizing it. When I saw the wild look in Mark's eyes, I realized those stories were true.

Bushed

Even men who are not lost can go crazy after spending too much time isolated in the bush. I never witnessed this "bushed" condition first hand until 1985, on a nineteen-day canoe trip on the Thelon River. The trip was scheduled during blackfly season, and it was clear from the outset that Jerry, an American from North Carolina, couldn't handle the bugs.

I provide headnets for my clients, and I make sure they all have the openings on their shirts closed off with Velcro. On this particular trip, the participants brought along their own bug jackets, as well. However, Jerry didn't have one and if ever anyone needed one, Jerry did. I never wear a bug jacket, but my wife sometimes did, so on the second day of the trip she gave hers to Jerry. Unfortunately, he lost it the very next day.

With each passing day, Jerry retreated steadily from social contact. His excuse was the bugs. After several days, Jerry was spending all of his time in camp inside his tent. He only came out to paddle in the bow of my canoe after we broke camp each morning. The only meal of the day he ate was lunch. By the end of the first week of the trip, it should have been clear that Jerry was headed for big trouble.

On the fourth-last day of the trip, Jerry burst into temper tantrums and became completely irrational. He acted like a three-year-old and we had to deal with him on that level. By then, he hadn't shaved or bathed in two weeks. He looked like a wild man. I remember one lunch near the end of the trip when Jerry rushed in to attack the food, stuffing his mouth with both hands like some half-starved wild animal. The rest of us just backed off and stared in disbelief.

On the third-last day of the trip Jerry refused to paddle. After much coaxing and threatening we managed to get him into the bow seat of my canoe where he sat in silence for hours with his arms crossed. Fortunately, I'm a strong paddler and we didn't have any big head winds.

When the float planes showed up on the last day of the trip, Jerry went berserk! As the first plane circled our campsite, he burst out of his tent—running, waving, jumping and shouting: "The plane, the plane, we're saved, we're saved!"

I've never seen anything like it, before or since.

A Dangerous Swim

It was a hot afternoon in August, and we were camped where a barrenland river funnelled down through a chute in a small canyon that we planned to portage the next morning. The river was squeezed to half its normal width by the canyon's sheer rock walls. The water was fast and full of standing waves, boils and whirlpools. So when Cam asked me if it was all right if he swam through this chute in the canyon, I replied with a firm no. It was a dangerous idea: there was a good chance he'd hit his head on a rock and drown.

I don't remember my precise words to Cam, but I know what was going through my mind. Safety is the first priority of every trip leader. Not only that, but if Cam died in that chute, we'd have to lug his body five miles up the river through several rapids and portages to a lake where a float plane could reach us, and once there we could sit for days trying to get a message out to our air charter company on my HF radio. At the same time, we'd have to deal with Cam's grieving wife. The trip would be over—for all of us. An accidental death would be tragic. It would also be bad for business.

I told Cam to stay out of the chute. I thought I had made myself very clear, but I had underestimated his thick-headedness. A few minutes later I heard him shout "Yahoo!" as he leaped off the canyon wall into the river. Several of our party were fishing in the pool below. They saw Cam come through and disappear underwater for what seemed to them as long as five minutes at the bottom of the chute. They didn't think he was going to resurface. It was probably less than minute, but in situations like that time seems to slow down. Cam finally came to the surface, uninjured. He was lucky to be alive.

I was steaming mad. If there had been satellite telephones in those days I would have expelled Cam from the trip as soon as I could get a plane there to pick him up. I doubt that Cam has ever realized how close he came to death that day. He has probably forgotten all about the incident. However, I've never forgotten it and I never will.

The Storm

Summers may be short in the Barren Lands, but they become longer, warmer and drier as you move inland away from the coasts. To someone like me, who grew up in the rather damp climate of eastern Canada, those dry, sunny summers are very appealing. With a climate as dry as Arizona's, the Barren Lands receive just four inches of rain per summer, yet few places on earth have as much water. This apparent paradox is a result of the brief arctic summer, which limits evaporation, as well as permafrost and the Canadian Shield, which greatly inhibit drainage.

Although big rainstorms can come along any time in the summer, they are more frequent in August, when summer changes to fall. Storms that appear quickly can be violent, but they never last long. Conversely, storms that move in slowly on big winds usually last much longer. In the Barren Lands, big rainstorms never end until the wind rotates counter-clockwise into the north and the temperature drops substantially.

Over the years, I've become more skilled at predicting when storms are imminent by observing cloud patterns as well as wind directions and velocities. Blackflies and loons also become much more active before a storm. The best indicator of all, however, is a barometer. I'm indebted to my good friend Kevin Antoniak, who made me a gift of one almost twenty years ago. Now, this little piece of technology is as important to me as my tent or sleeping bag. I wouldn't be caught without it.

When a storm is brewing, the important thing is to avoid getting pinned down in an exposed location. I always take my group to cover in a clump of trees or, if none are present, behind a hill or an esker. In August, when the insects are gone, I make a habit of camping every night in a location where we will be protected from the north and the east.

As in all other aspects of conducting my canoe trips, I live by my three cardinal rules in anticipation of bad weather: (1) be prepared; (2) never take chances; and (3) remember that Mother Nature is always in charge, and her power on the wide open tundra can be an awesome thing. You have to learn to bend like the willow before the wind. You have to know when to hide.

The big storm that roared in over much of western and northern Canada in late June of 1999 caught meteorologists by surprise, I'm told. I don't know why that would be so, because I was pretty sure something big and bad was coming days beforehand. My clients and I were canoeing in the southern Barrens. Five days before the storm struck, the weather became hot, muggy and dead calm. The barometric pressure fell into the basement and stayed there. With calm, clear weather and temperatures in the 80s and 90s (Fahrenheit), I couldn't hole up, even though I was certain a storm was on its way. I had no other option but to keep travelling, keep an eye on the sky and try to camp in a protected place each night. On the second-last night of our canoe trip I wrote in my diary that I hoped we'd get out of there before the hammer fell. We didn't. The hammer fell the next morning.

The mood of the Barren Lands is like that of the little girl "with the curl in the middle of her forehead." When she's good she's very good, but when she's bad she's horrid. We were about to find out how horrid she could get. By noon the next day we were experiencing heavy rain and gale-force winds. Although the land around us was flat, open tundra with little to break the wind, our tents were pitched adjacent to a small clump of black spruce growing eight or ten feet in height. This little spruce grove provided a welcome place to get out of the storm. I cooked our meals in there with a canoe braced up on its side as an added windbreak for our stove. All was well when we crawled into our sleeping bags that night.

All night long the wind and heavy rain pounded our tents. By the time I arose the next morning some of the things inside my tent were starting to get wet. When I peeked out of the door I was shocked to see two of our six tents flat on the ground. My own tent was secure, but I had reset the pegs before I had gone to bed. I made my way over to one of the flattened tents, which was squarely in the middle of a big puddle of water. Much to my surprise, Tom and Barb were still inside and apparently all right.

While Tom and Barb got dressed, I returned to my tent to call the air charter company in Fort Smith. The planes were supposed to arrive by ten that morning, but visibility was down to less than half a mile. There was no way an airplane could fly in this stuff. I got on my satellite telephone, gave our pilots the news and told them I'd keep them posted. The weather wasn't much better in Fort Smith.

The next order of the day was to re-erect the two flattened tents. Our tents were four-season geodesic domes with vestibules, only four feet high and anchored down with twenty-seven pegs apiece. They could stand up to one hell of a wind. I'd been using this model of nylon tent for quite a few years, and I'd never seen one flattened before.

Our location on the lee shore of a small lake was the best

campsite around for miles. Although the topography was gently rolling with little shelter, we were on a well-drained bench of sand nicely covered with tundra vegetation. Normally, such tent sites would see us through the worst of times, but this was shaping up to be something a little beyond that.

The real problem was the continuing, heavy rain. The ground was completely saturated, and that, combined with the high winds, meant the pegs could no longer hold on to the tents very effectively. Once the pegs on the windward guy lines gave way, the tents could be blown flat on the ground. If we could have replaced those pegs with rocks, the problem would have been solved. However, we were camped in one of those unusual places where no rocks were handy.

Tom and Barb's tent, though undamaged, was so wet that we just stuffed it into a pack and moved them into two other tents. Most of the tents held two occupants, but could sleep four in a pinch, so there was easily enough room to add another person to each. The spare tent I always carry was no help because the wind and rain were driving so hard that there wasn't any chance of getting it up successfully.

So much rain had fallen by the second morning of the storm that the tundra was turning into a giant swamp. Caribou trails had become creeks. There were streams capable of floating loaded canoes where only dry ground had been before. Pools of water lay everywhere. In fact, a lot of those pools were ponds. Our protective grove of spruce was now flooded out, part of a newborn stream that roared across the beach and into the lake we were camped on. The lake itself was rising steadily.

I was able to cook breakfast that morning, thanks to the thicket of black spruce that still sheltered what was left of a strand of sand beach along the lake. However, the beach was disappearing rapidly. Our tents were getting wet from underneath, so we dug trenches around each one to carry the water away. This was the first time in my life I had ever trenched a tent.

That afternoon, the wind shifted into the north and the rain changed to snow. The wind continued at gale-force velocities and the snow began to accumulate. Late that afternoon, I cleared over a foot of snow off the windward sides of the tents. Somehow, I managed to cook supper again that night. I always carry three extra days of food, so there was plenty to eat. Although no one was very dry or comfortable, we all got through the night reasonably well and without any complaints.

Everyone's travel schedule was now in jeopardy. Our chartered aircraft couldn't even leave Fort Smith that day, let alone reach us in the Barrens. This was the first time in my guiding career that we had failed to return to Fort Smith on our predesignated date. But then, this storm was producing a lot of firsts. All of my clients were ticketed to fly out of Fort Smith to Edmonton at one o'clock the next afternoon, but it was pretty clear now that they would miss their flight. On my satellite telephone that night I learned the weather was improving in Fort Smith, and I was reasonably confident the weather would get better where we were the next day as well.

By seven the next morning, the storm had eased considerably. The wind was down and the snow had changed back to rain. When I telephoned our air charter company, Doug Williamson told me he thought he could reach us later that morning. At noon, just as the last of the rain fell, the float planes swooped in from Fort Smith. We sure were glad to see them. In the previous forty-eight hours somewhere between three and six inches of rain and snow had fallen. Water lay everywhere. Our lake had risen four feet and was still rising. In my thirty summers in the Barren Lands I've seen some bad storms, and certainly some that have lasted much longer, but this was the worst of them all.

The Big Wind

In the North, there are strong summer winds; we never experience tornadoes, but small cyclones or whirlwinds are not uncommon. I've seen corridors through the bush where one of these wind funnels has flattened a swath of trees, and once when I was on a solo canoe trip a whirlwind ripped across a small lake in front of me, raising a frightening waterspout at least fifty feet high. A few years ago I got some idea of what it might be like if one of those whirlwinds actually struck you out on the water.

We had just made our final camp on the Thelon River. Our float planes were due to pick us up the next morning. It was thunderstorm weather: a hot, still afternoon with big dark clouds some distance away, but moving steadily in on us. Just before the wind whipped up, there was an unusual straight line in those clouds. If I ever see a line like that again, I'll recognize it for what it is—big trouble.

I don't know if the wind that slammed us that afternoon was a whirlwind or a wind shear, but whatever it was, it was by far the most violent wind I have ever experienced. It only lasted a few minutes, but it tore our camp apart.

It had been a quiet afternoon up to that point. We had overturned, but not tied down, our five canoes on a rock beach about thirty yards from the edge of the river. The beach ran along beside the river for about a quarter of a mile and ended on a sharp bend. My own canoe is twenty feet long and weighs 110 pounds. Nonetheless, the wind picked up all of those canoes like bits of paper and flew them down the full length of the rock beach, with only one or two touchdowns, before tossing them into the river.

The Thelon is fast at that point and, luckily for us, the canoes all rolled over in the river with the wind and filled up with water. We found them another half mile downstream, washed up against an outside bend on our side of the river.

It always pays to have the best equipment! That tumble down the rock beach would have broken lesser canoes, but mine are constructed of Royalex, the toughest and most flexible material on today's market. Apart from a few scrapes and two broken bolts on one thwart, there was no significant damage except to my twenty-footer, which suffered a small hole. All we had to do was empty them out and portage them back into camp. It only took minutes to make a permanent repair on the twenty-footer and it was none the worse for wear.

Respect

In the Barren Lands I always conduct myself with the feeling that the spirits of the ancient aboriginal peoples—and even my own ancestors—are looking down on me, constantly scrutinizing my behaviour. To some degree, I feel my fate rests in the hands of these spirits so I must conduct myself appropriately. Next to the safety of my clients, my highest priority is to ensure that my parties always treat the pristine tundra wilderness with the utmost respect.

Respect for the land means leaving it the way you found it. For me, that means coming as close as I can to no-trace camping. All of my garbage goes back to town, including paper. I depackage most of my food beforehand anyway, so there's very little waste. Until recently, I built little stone fireplaces, where I cooked on a grill. I used only small sticks of wood that burned down to ash without leaving charcoal. Now I cook everything on a stove. The only things my clients and I leave behind are our tracks in the sand. After a few weeks, anyone following us would never know we had been there.

Most canoeists are reasonably respectful of the Barren Lands. Almost all of them carry out or burn their refuse. Except for aluminium foil packaging in some canoeists' fireplaces, I very rarely see any garbage, even on such well-travelled rivers as the Thelon. Unfortunately, many government personnel, some air charter companies and the mining industry are much less respectful. The junk they abandon dwarfs that of all other sources combined. The most common eyesores are brightly coloured, forty-five-gallon fuel barrels. There's no escaping them. They're almost everywhere, and they float down rivers on spring floods for hundreds of miles.

It is with fire that canoeists commit their greatest sins. Considering the small numbers of people canoeing in the Canadian Arctic, I see far too many ugly fire scars above the high-water mark along the rivers and lakes. In this cold climate these scars take decades to heal. When I used small cooking fires, I always built them well below the high-water mark close to the water's edge. If others did the same, their fire scars would be scoured clean by the next spring flood.

Europeans are the worst culprits with fire. Living where they do, few Europeans have an opportunity to develop any camping skills. When they come to the remote Canadian wilderness they must feel that they have arrived on another planet. Perhaps Europeans are so intimidated by absolute wilderness that they turn to fire to soothe their fears. Whatever the reason, most Europeans who go canoeing in our North seem to build fires almost every time they go ashore. Invariably, they cut down and burn green trees in big blazes that produce large quantities of charcoal and partially burned logs. Some of these disgusting messes ruin campsites for many of us for decades to come. Since fire is subject to so much abuse by inexperienced campers, if it were up to me, I would abolish its use everywhere.

Larry's Inuit Graves

The North is full of interesting archaeological sites of stone-age man. In the Barren Lands we often make surface finds of spearpoints, arrowheads, stone knives and scrapers of Indian origin that are thousands of years old. In places, there are rows of "stone men"—rocks stacked on top of each other a few feet high—that sometimes stretch for a mile or more at traditional caribou crossings along the major rivers or at narrow places between large lakes. These are the remains of caribou fences that were once used to direct the herds to strategic ambush locations. Higher, windswept places are where we find stone tent rings. It was in places like these that ancient peoples watched for the summer caribou migrations while minimizing their exposure to biting insects.

More recent evidence of Chipewyan Dene includes woodwork, ranging from the remains of old birchwood toboggans to birchbark canoes. Tipi poles are also commonly seen just north of the forest. I know of one little clump of spruce trees about fifty miles north of treeline that contains hundreds of tipi poles dating back to the 1800s. The climate is so cold and dry that wood seems to last forever. Birchbark probably endures for hundreds of years in the Barren Lands. I've often found small rolls of birchbark peppered with tiny holes along their edges that were hundreds of miles out on the tundra in places like Beverly Lake.

In eastern sections of the central Barrens we have found many archaeological sites of the Inuit. Since these sites are no older than the late 1800s, they're more elaborate and better preserved than the sites of ancient Indian cultures. There are caribou fences, clusters of tent rings, kayak stands, impressive meat caches, hunting blinds, chipping sites, projectile points, stone tools and various kinds of well-preserved wooden objects. Then, of course, there are the famous *inuksuit*: usually big, solitary stacks of rocks built by the Inuit as markers to guide them on their travels; they are quite unlike the rows of smaller stone men that serve as caribou fences. I've seen *inuksuit* up to ten feet in height, containing hundreds of stones. (*Inuksuit* is the plural of *inuksuk*, meaning "likeness of man.")

The Thelon River is especially rich in archaeological sites of both Indian and Inuit origin. Many prominent hilltops along the middle Thelon contain truckloads of quartzite chips where ancient caribou hunters once fashioned points and blades while they waited for the herds to appear. At ambush sites and near tent rings we often find arrowheads, spearpoints and knives. In fact, on all of my regular canoe routes in the Barren Lands, we've found at least some of this kind of archaeological material. Because it's illegal to remove any of these artifacts, they stay where we've found them for successive groups of my clients to enjoy year after year.

South of treeline, I have found many Dene graves of varying age. The oldest ones are simply the remains of log rectangles at ground level—sometimes with four fallen javelin-shaped corner posts and collapsed log roofs. More modern Dene graves have crosses or picket fences. Always, they are in high places that look out over rivers and lakes.

Despite the relative abundance of Dene graves in the taiga, I was never convinced that my clients and I had ever found a grave of any kind on the tundra until Larry joined one of my Thelon River trips in 1982. Larry was a young lawyer from California who had brought his twelve-year-old stepdaughter, Amanda, with him. Amanda was a wonderful young girl and very mature for her age. We used to joke that it was Amanda who took care of Larry, instead of the other way around.

With a day to spare at the end of the trip, we roamed the tundra at Beverly Lake in search of archaeological sites, which abound in that particular area. We managed to find a few small *inuksuit*, some hunting blinds and meat caches, but nothing more exotic than that. The next night I was sitting next to Larry in a restaurant in Fort Smith enjoying a final dinner with my group of clients. It was then that Larry confessed to me that he'd wandered off by himself the day before at Beverly Lake and had discovered the remains of a large Inuit camp, including several graves where human skulls and various artifacts were visible.

I was surprised that no one else in our party had found Larry's graves, because most of us had spent the whole day exploring the general area, while Larry had never ventured far from camp. When I asked Larry why he hadn't shared his find with the rest of us, he declared he was so overwhelmed by what he had seen that he wasn't able to speak of it at the time. Although I thought his explanation was rather strange, it wasn't entirely out of character for Larry. I resolved to find Larry's Inuit graves when I returned to Beverly Lake the next summer.

A year later we did, indeed, find ourselves at the same campsite at Beverly Lake, with a day to spare before the float planes picked us up to return us to Fort Smith. Larry had been vague about the exact location of the graves, but there wasn't a tree around for miles and I thought it would be easy enough to locate them. Our party organized itself, and we spent the entire day scouring the tundra for miles around, but we failed to locate the elusive Inuit graves.

It wasn't until the next winter, when I was chatting on the telephone with one of my clients, that the riddle was solved to my satisfaction. This client had been on the same trip as Larry two summers before. When I told him about our failure to turn up the Inuit graves, he offered some information about Larry that I hadn't known. According to my client, Larry had spent every night of the trip in his tent stoned on marijuana. The Inuit graves were nothing more than a figment of Larry's intoxicated mind.

PART III

The Wildlife

The Ways of the Caribou

Caribou are nearly always on the move, going somewhere, even if nowhere in particular. There's still a lot of truth in an old Dene saying: "No one knows the ways of the wind and the caribou." However, there are three broad patterns of caribou movements that are largely predictable: the spring, summer and fall migrations.

In the late winter and spring, caribou migrate from winter ranges, which are usually in the forest, to summer ranges, which are always on the tundra. The pregnant cows and most of their surviving calves from the previous year travel directly to the calving grounds, sometimes more than four hundred miles away. The bulls, the barren cows and some young often lag hundreds of miles behind. Although the calving grounds can shift over time, they occupy the same general geographic location year after year and are usually near the edge of each herd's home range, far out on the tundra. Almost all of the calves in a herd are born within a few days of each other in early June. This is probably a defence mechanism against predators. The glut of calves appearing all at once limits the overall predation by attendant wolves and grizzlies.

For some caribou herds, like the Beverly and Bathurst herds, the post-calving movements are a full-fledged summer migration spanning hundreds of miles. This summer migration begins in June after the calves are born and generally terminates at treeline in the last week of July or the first week of August, but sometimes later. It is less direct and often less rapid than the spring migration, especially in its earlier stages. During the later stages, herds of bulls sometimes precede the cows and calves, but often, both sexes and all age classes are well mixed in large herds that can sometimes comprise over 100,000 animals. As they approach the treeline, these large herds fragment, and for most of August caribou are widely dispersed north of the forest in small groups containing fewer than thirty animals. Aggregations of hundreds or even thousands of caribou are sometimes found near treeline later in August, but this is exceptional. The bulls often occupy different areas than the cows and calves and are usually found farther south. In my experience, caribou rarely enter the continuous forest at this time of year. On the contrary, large numbers drift north again in August and September, farther out on the tundra.

The fall migration begins in October or early November during or just after the rut. It becomes strongly directional and rapid, straight into the forest, and usually terminates on winter ranges in early December.

Although the precise routes and timing of caribou migrations are unpredictable, there are broad migration corridors that tend to be used much more frequently than adjacent areas. These corridors are evident from the number of caribou trails through them. The most frequently used migration routes follow along the lines of least topographical resistance. Movements along chains of frozen lakes, along the tops of eskers and glacial ridges, and parallel to major watersheds are most common. Even though caribou are incredibly strong swimmers and sometimes strike out across miles of open water, they most often cross rivers and lakes at their narrowest points or via a chain of islands.

Throughout the 1980s, the Beverly caribou herd crossed the lower Hanbury and middle Thelon rivers in nearly all the same places and on virtually the same dates in late July, year after year. It got so that I could predict where they would be almost to the day, and I routed my canoe trips accordingly. However, caribou have a way of humbling you when you are getting too cocky. In the 1990s, the Beverly herd's summer migration routes and their timing kept shifting and no predictable patterns were discernible.

When caribou migrate in numbers they create trails. The Barren Lands and northernmost parts of the forest are carved up with billions of these trails. In many areas, one cannot take more than a few steps without coming upon a caribou trail of some kind. Often, eskers and hillsides are terraced with hundreds of caribou trails paralleling each other only a foot or two apart. Although the most commonly used trails are worn deep into the tundra and may be thousands of years old, new caribou trails can be created in a matter of minutes.

Tundra vegetation is fragile and cannot withstand much trampling. Although it doesn't become apparent for another week or two, a handful of canoeists will begin to kill the tundra plants in the most frequently trodden parts of their campsite over the course of a single day. Because caribou tend to migrate in lines, with the animal behind following in the footsteps of the one in front, just a few hundred caribou can create a typical eight-inch-wide trail. I have often come along a few weeks after a major caribou migration has passed by and been struck by the new trails in the form of narrow, brown ribbons of dead vegetation.

Caribou migrations are often clearly led by cows. These are probably some of the oldest and most experienced females in the herd.

Large numbers of migrating caribou will often pile up at a major water crossing, sometimes for a day or more. Invariably, it seems to be some old cow that finally plunges into the water and leads the way, with the entire herd strung out behind her.

I remember one warm, breezy evening on the Thelon late in July when my wife, Lia, and I climbed up on top of the esker we were camped on for one last look around before going to bed. A couple of miles away we noticed the fine sand along the esker billowing up into the air like smoke. Within minutes, a densely packed column of caribou appeared along the top of the esker. When the cows in the vanguard were about thirty paces from us, they stopped abruptly, bringing the entire mile-long column to a halt. After a few minutes of eyeing us blocking their path, one cow finally took a ninety-degree turn down off the esker. Twenty thousand animals followed her into the valley below.

Caribou may be the most studied animal in the North, but to my mind they are still the most mysterious. They seem to need huge areas of wilderness in order to thrive. Their population swings and the whys, hows, wheres and whens of their great annual migrations are still poorly understood. As another old Dene saying goes: "Caribou are like ghosts; they come from nowhere, fill up all the land, then disappear."

Guardians of the Gates

Bugs—blackflies and mosquitoes—may be very small inhabitants of the tundra, but they have a very big reputation. That reputation is built on their numbers. In fact, the Barren Lands may have the densest populations of blackflies on earth.

There's probably more weight in living matter bound up in biting insects on the tundra than in all other forms of life combined. It's the fear of this winged and biting scourge that keeps people out of the Barren Lands. The stories and myths are legion.

Some of my clients will only consider a canoe trip in August, when insects are minimal or almost absent. By limiting their options to August, those clients are missing out on twenty-four-hour daylight, the best weather of the summer and my finest wildlife trips. It's true, the bugs can be bad in late June and most certainly in July, but even at peak numbers, the wind usually keeps them away, especially on the water. The tundra is windy country where there's little to stop the wind. Evenings, after the wind has died, are when the insects get troublesome.

Unlike mosquitoes, blackflies lay their eggs in moving water. They hatch out of big rapids in enormous numbers. As a barrenland canoeist, you soon learn to camp in exposed locations that are distant from rapids during the blackfly season; you learn the value of headnets, of staying clean, of wearing light-coloured clothing, of closing the openings on your shirts with Velcro and of locating your camp kitchens out on rock bars, as far away from vegetation as possible. You also learn that unlike mosquitoes, blackflies won't bite you inside your tent. However, the most valuable lesson you'll ever learn when it comes to dealing with biting insects is developing the right kind of attitude. It has a lot to do with mind over matter.

Blackflies are least bothersome when the barometric pressure is high. They are much more active on warm, cloudy, windless days and they work themselves into an absolute frenzy before a storm. I always keep a barometer hung inside my tent, but even without it, I can usually tell when a rainstorm is on the way. The loons start calling and the blackflies get bloodthirsty.

Blackflies are only active within a fairly narrow range of temperature. They become very lethargic when the temperature exceeds 85°F and at 46°F they simply shut down and disappear. Blackflies are also inactive in the dark, but that's a condition we never experience on the Barrens during the peak of blackfly season.

Mosquitoes hatch out long before blackflies and disappear first. When the leaves come out, so do the mosquitoes. Blackflies don't begin to appear until after mosquitoes have reached peak populations. Once the blackflies begin to emerge, they are only really numerous for about three weeks. If summer comes early, so do the insects, and hot, dry summers are hard on them. During these kinds of summers, tundra areas within one hundred miles of treeline are sometimes free of biting insects as early as mid-July. Late summers, on the other hand, delay the emergence of insects. During the unusually cold summer of 1978, blackflies didn't appear along the middle Thelon River until the end of July, at least two weeks later than normal.

Because the timing of the blackfly hatch is a function of the severity of the climate, blackflies appear later in the season as you proceed deeper into the tundra, away from treeline. For example, blackflies may begin to emerge in late June near treeline, but two hundred miles out on the tundra, their emergence may be delayed for another month. This variation in the timing of blackfly cycles across the Barren Lands is exploited by the Beverly and Bathurst caribou herds in their summer migration to treeline, which they time beautifully to minimize their insect exposure. It's my belief that this migration evolved as an escape from blackflies.

For example, the Beverly caribou herd stays in the northernmost part of its range, far out on the tundra, during the early summer, when blackflies are hatching further south. The southward migration begins before the blackflies emerge in these northernmost areas. The migration is timed to cross the Hanbury and Thelon rivers in mid-July or shortly thereafter, just as blackflies usually start to appear in large numbers. At this point in the migration, most caribou are travelling in herds of thousands, tens of thousands or even hundreds of thousands. The advantage of staying in big, closely packed herds is that insect harassment of individual caribou is kept to an absolute minimum.

The Beverly caribou keep moving south until they reach treeline, usually sometime during the first week of August. As they approach treeline, they enter areas where both mosquitoes and blackflies have already gone through their cycles and have largely disappeared. Now the big herds break up into small groups and disperse over huge areas north of the forest, slowing down and beginning to fatten.

If you're a barrenland canoeist and you want to escape the worst of the blackflies, you try to do as the caribou do. Unfortunately, it's not that easy. For one thing, most river systems in the Barrens flow north, not south. The breakup of ice on rivers and lakes progresses in a northerly direction as well. There are simply not many areas far out on the tundra where ice conditions will permit you to canoe very far early in the season. And during the last two weeks of July it's often difficult to avoid blackflies no matter where you are.

Around the end of July, there's a very large subspecies of blackfly that emerges in unbelievable numbers in some locations. Thankfully, I've only encountered this subspecies on a few occasions. One of those was some years ago on the Back River, where my clients and I were camped one night. The blackflies were so thick that there were actually layers of them covering my clothing. I remember preparing supper under these conditions while my clients hid in their tents, afraid to come out. I moved around stiffly and deliberately, as if I was wearing a suit of armour. If I bent an arm or leg too far I would crush thousands of blackflies against my clothing. One of my frequent clients still likes to rib me about that evening because when I had supper ready I called out to the others in their tents, "Come and get it, you cowards!"

The first time I became aware of this large subspecies of blackfly was in 1974, near the end of a canoe trip that lasted most of the summer. Peter Griffiths and I had just come ashore on Aberdeen Lake on the lower Thelon River when we were greeted by clouds of these insects. Their numbers were so great that they quite literally obscured our vision. We decided to skip supper and eat some snacks in our tent instead. We had a white Egyptian cotton tent and I recall that after we had pitched it, the blackflies began rolling down it in waves as if a living fountain of them sprang from its peak. Our white tent soon became quite black.

After Peter and I had erected our tent, the trick was to get into it without the bugs. As all barrenland canoeists know, that's usually not very difficult to do. Blackflies don't fly very fast and you can certainly outrun them. To shed your swarm of blackflies, you first walk about a hundred yards away from your tent, preferably downwind if there's a breeze. Next you run around and shake, brush and swat the blackflies off your clothing. Then you run like hell to your tent and try to get through the zipper on the door as fast as you can. Under most conditions, you'll end up with no more than a few dozen blackflies in your tent. This procedure works effectively on mosquitoes as well.

On that bug-infested evening on Aberdeen Lake, Peter was first to shake off his blackflies and run to the tent. Once inside, he operated the tent door zipper so I could make a faster entry by diving through. Despite our best efforts, some blackflies managed to follow us into our tent, partly on our clothing and partly by flying through the door during those few seconds it was open. Just for laughs, we decided to count the blackflies inside our tent. We killed them with a few shots of insecticide and swept them into a pile on the floor. We each took a piece of the pile and counted carcasses. Then we estimated what fraction of the pile we had counted and came up with the approximate number of blackflies that had entered our tent. It was fifty thousand!

White Wolves of the Tundra

By anyone's definition, a place that sustains wolverines or grizzlies has to be wilderness. Most people would add wolves to that list, but of the three, the wolf is the most tolerant of man. That shouldn't be surprising, because for thousands of years domesticated wolves, or dogs as we call them, have been known as man's best friend. I, for one, consider the wolf to be the most fascinating animal on our continent simply because it is the most intelligent and socially advanced animal next to us. Also like us, wolves have individual personalities and express emotions that we as humans can easily intuit.

Wolf society is extremely well organized. The basic social unit is the pack, which exists because wolves need to co-operate with one another in order to kill prey that is usually faster, larger or stronger than they are. The pack is essentially an extended family, organized in a hierarchy that is usually dominated by the breeding male. More than one female capable of breeding may be present within this family group, but seldom is more than one litter of pups produced. Nevertheless, all members of the pack co-operate in hunting large prey and in feeding and guarding the young.

Wolves are able to regulate their own numbers in relation to the available food and space. This is accomplished through social mechanisms that not only limit the number of litters produced, but also control litter sizes and the survival of pups. The result is that unexploited wolf populations maintain relatively stable numbers and most pups die at an early age.

Unlike other races of wolves, tundra wolves are nomadic. They follow their staff of life, the great caribou herds, on their annual migrations from the Barren Lands to the subarctic forests and back each winter. Only during the denning period, from about mid-May to late August, are the breeding packs prevented from roaming with their prey and confined to the vicinity of their dens.

In the spring, few wolves follow the caribou all the way to the calving grounds. The great majority drop off, some as far back as treeline, to dig their dens and raise their pups. Tundra wolves may even precede the caribou to their denning areas, especially if the spring caribou migration is late getting started. The wolves' strategy of denning short of the calving grounds increases their chances of having caribou available to them during the denning period. Nevertheless, caribou may be out of reach for much of the summer, particularly near treeline, which can result in food shortages and high mortality rates among wolf pups. When caribou are absent, the wolves are forced to fall back on other prey (from voles to moose), which can seldom sustain them for any length of time. Recent increases in moose and muskox populations near treeline, however, could now be contributing substantial benefits to the wolves that den in these more southern areas.

Tundra wolves come in a variety of colours. They can be grey, brown, tawny or even coal black, but over 80 percent are white or whitish. This is a medium-sized wolf that can weigh up to 140 pounds. Ninety pounds is average. Pack size is fairly small. Never have I encountered more than six adults together during the summer, and most of my wolf sightings have been of single animals. Obviously, most tundra wolves hunt alone in the summer and they are certainly capable of catching and killing caribou without the benefit of other pack members.

The pups are usually born in late May or early June, although some litters appear considerably later. After their first three weeks of life, the pups spend a fair amount of time above ground, sleeping and playing near the entrances to their den, which usually serves as a focal point of activity for the entire pack until sometime in August. Tundra wolves will often move their pups from the den to a "rendezvous site," but rarely do so before the end of July. By late August, the pups are usually old enough to follow the pack to some extent in their nomadic pursuit of the caribou herds. You'll seldom find tundra wolves and their pups at a den past the middle of August and never, in my experience, later than the end of that month.

Wolf dens are surprisingly clean and odourless, with very few bones in the area. The adults feed the pups by regurgitating food for them.

Each pack appears to have several denning sites for raising its pups. The pack may rotate the use of specific dens from one year to the next or move the pups from one den to another if they are disturbed. Some denning sites are occupied several years in succession. The first wolf den I found on the Thelon River in 1971 was active with pups in eleven of the sixteen years I visited it before it was flooded out in 1991. Another den I know of on the Thelon has been occupied for sixteen of the past nineteen years. Key denning sites could be hundreds of years old, or even far older.

At one traditional den on the Thelon, I recognized the same pair of wolves every summer for a number of years. We used to have a little trick we played on each other. I'd camp with my clients upriver from the den, then visit it in the late afternoon. That night, the adults would move the pups to another den a mile downriver. The next morning we'd paddle down to the second den for another experience with the same wolves. We kept this little game up for quite a few years until the second den was dug up by a grizzly that tried, unsuccessfully, to make a meal of the pups.

One of the most attractive features of tundra wolves is their boldness and curiosity. In the Barren Lands, where man is a stranger, wolves will often approach people quite closely. I often think the sight of our tents out on the open tundra must pique the curiosity of wolves. I have videotape of tundra wolves walking into our campsites, within six feet of my clients, looking in the doors of our tents and sniffing the pots and pans in our camp kitchens—obviously curious, obviously unafraid, and quite innocent and unaggressive.

One encounter with a curious wolf that stands out in my memory occurred on one of our canoe trips on the Back River. We were camped on the upper Back, an extremely rocky area of tundra where tent sites were very much at a premium. Our half dozen tents were pitched so close together that the guy lines of adjacent tents crisscrossed each other. It was a bug-infested night, so after we had eaten our supper everyone went to bed early, while I washed up the pots and dishes at the edge of the river. The evening was so quiet that I could plainly hear my clients talking in their tents up on the tundra.

After finishing my chores, I noticed a beautiful white wolf sitting right smack in the middle of our crowd of tents. The wolf hadn't spotted me, so I watched as its attention turned from one voice to another as the chatter and laughter shifted back and forth between the occupants of the various tents. It was as if the wolf was enjoying the conversation. There was clearly curiosity and intelligence there, and it that struck me as almost human.

There's a human-like quality in the way wolves play, as well. Last summer, my clients and I happened upon six adult wolves and four pups that were completely unaware of us watching them at their rendezvous site. Some of the adults must have just returned from a lengthy hunt, because there was a great deal of vocalizing and running around. The pups were chasing the adults and soliciting food, while other adults wrestled and chased each other as if they were playing a game of tag.

We watched their good-natured horseplay at close quarters for the better part of an hour. In my mind's eye I still have the image of a big white wolf standing over a black one, which lay on its back with its legs straight up in the air. Both of them wore laugh-like grins. There was a real joie de vivre in that family of wolves that testified to their intelligence and affection for each other.

Aboriginal peoples have always recognized the intelligence of wolves and traditionally treated them as special creatures. Samuel Hearne, the first great European explorer of the Barren Lands, declared that the Chipewyan Dene held the wolf in such high esteem that few of them would kill one "under the notion that they were something more than common animals." These were the same people who Hearne claimed "were so accustomed to kill everything that came within their reach that few of them could pass by a small bird's nest without slaying the young ones or destroying the eggs." Yet Hearne wrote that he frequently saw these Dene go to wolf dens "and take out the young ones and play with them. I never knew a Northern Indian [Chipewyan] to hurt one of them; on the contrary, they always put them carefully into the den again." (My clients and I have done the same.)

When I was working on wolves for my master's degree at the University of Toronto, Clive Elliot, one of our team members studying wolf behaviour on Baffin Island, told me of an experience that suggests some extraordinary aspects of the intelligence of the wolf. Clive and the rest of the research team were camped close to a wolf den and daily observed and recorded the activities of the adults and their pups. One female, which they had nicknamed Brownie, was like a big, friendly dog, and periodically visited them at their campsite. Early one morning when the young biologists were all sound asleep in their big wall tent, Brownie slipped into camp and bit through the tent's supporting guy ropes, collapsing the whole works on top of its unsuspecting occupants. When Clive finally managed to struggle free, he spotted Brownie sitting on her haunches a short way off. Clive swears she wore a wide grin.

Unlike the shyer timber wolf of more southern forested regions, the tundra wolf is an animal that is frequently seen. The absence of trees and the conspicuous white colouration of most tundra wolves play a role in this, of course, but so do the curiosity and bold innocence of the animal itself. Since the 1970s, I have seen over one thousand tundra wolves in my travels. I have also found over eighty of their dens. The majority of my wolf sightings and my most memorable experiences have occurred at those dens. The key to seeing wolves in the Barren Lands lies in finding wolf dens and in visiting as many of those dens as often as possible. I've been visiting one den on an annual basis, though it has never been active since I found it in 1986. I keep visiting it because I believe that one of these years it will produce a wonderful experience for my clients and me. I can think of several dens that were reoccupied by wolves after an absence of six or seven years. Persistence pays off.

Active wolf dens are actually quite easy to find. Sometimes I stumble on them by accident, but usually I find them by following a progression of clues. The trick is to capitalize on chance encounters with wolves to lead you to their dens—but you have to know what to look for.

Key initial clues can be found in the behaviour of the wolf and the type of soil in the area. Since wolf dens are substantial holes in the ground, wolves need to choose soils where the digging is easy and where permafrost lies a good distance below the surface. On the Barrens, this usually means sandy areas. Eskers are especially favoured. All of the big eskers that snake their way across the Barren Lands are well populated by denning wolves. I once found three dens with pups along a seventeen-mile stretch of esker.

When they're on babysitting duty at a den, adult wolves seem to spend most of their time sleeping. A sleeping wolf in or close to a sandy area is a good reason to suspect there may be a den nearby. Two or more and it's almost a certainty. If I see lots of tracks when I inspect sandy areas or if I encounter a wolf that seems secretive or follows me at a distance, I'll keep searching. If a wolf howls at me, I know I'm getting closer, and barking is a dead giveaway. I've only heard wolves bark when I was close to their dens. The density or direction of tracks in the sand may lead me closer.

Wolf dens are usually located on the south side of a sandy hill, esker, ravine or small hummock of some kind. Even out on the tundra, wolves usually dig their dens under spruce trees if any are available. The roots prevent the dens from collapsing and help protect the pups from being dug out by grizzlies. Water, even if it's only a small pond, is nearly always close by. When I come upon an area containing a lot of wolf scat, I can be sure I am within a few hundred yards of a den. This is a loafing area for the adult wolves guarding the pups.

Once I have located a wolf den, I keep my clients quiet and we approach from downwind in order to maximize our opportunities for close-up encounters with the adults and pups. I've frequently walked up to within a few feet of wolves asleep at their den, then whistled to awaken them for a photograph. Often, the pups are out of sight, deep inside the den. If that's the case, I'll usually wait quietly downwind for at least fifteen minutes. Sometimes my patience is rewarded. If the pups fail to materialize, I find that a few fake wolf howls often bring a pup or two out for a look. If there are any adults inside the den, they'll come out immediately upon hearing me howl.

Sometimes, the pups will be sleeping some distance away from the safety of their den. If there are dwarf birch, willow or spruce thickets in the vicinity, I always check them out. Doing so has produced a lot of wolf pup sightings for me over the years.

Pups up to six or seven weeks old can't run very fast and are easy to catch away from their dens. Once they're in hand, they become quite docile and as easy to handle as their domestic brethren. Wolves never reject their young after they have been handled by humans. They're much too intelligent to react in that way. To my mind, there's nothing more adorable than a three-to-five-week-old, fat, fuzzy wolf puppy with its oversize feet. The privilege of holding a wolf pup is usually the pinnacle of my clients' canoe trips.

A wolf den I once found on the Thelon River will serve as a good example of how I typically find active dens by following a series of clues. My clients and I had just set up our camp for the night when we decided to go for a walk together downriver. We soon came upon two big holes in the side of the riverbank and noticed a few fresh wolf tracks on the beach below. The scarcity of tracks indicated this wasn't a den containing pups, but I had often seen holes like this in the vicinity of whelping dens before.

We were just climbing back up the riverbank when I spotted a white wolf walking straight towards us. I motioned for the others to stay down until the wolf was close. When I gave the signal we all stood up with our cameras at the ready. But instead of showing alarm, the wolf simply stared at us, then casually retreated to the side of a nearby hill where it curled up and watched us.

The periodic howling of wolves throughout the night confirmed for me that there was a den in the area, so after breakfast the following morning we set out in search of it. When a big, sandy stand of spruce trees behind our campsite failed to produce many tracks, we walked further inland along a small, stony esker. A half mile farther on, we came upon an old caved-in wolf den. As we were looking it over, one of our group spotted what appeared to be the same wolf we'd seen the day before, standing on a hilltop some distance away. After the wolf and I traded some howls, the wolf came running towards us, but angled off as it approached.

I was now certain we were heading in the right direction and that seemed to be confirmed when some sand dunes soon came into view. There, we found a line of tracks going back and forth, suggesting the comings and goings of wolves around a den. The tracks led us to the edge of a small lake where we found a maze of wolf prints, a few well-chewed caribou bones and wolf scats everywhere. It was obvious that the den was very close by.

I finally spotted a hole in the side of a small, sandy hummock, just as the white wolf and a light grey one appeared on a hill behind us and began to howl. I slowly crept up to the den entrance and peeked inside. No animals were visible, but there were two more holes on top of the hummock so I climbed up to investigate. Meanwhile, Lia, with the rest of our party strung out behind her, moved up to the first entrance.

Suddenly, I heard Lia yell! She was only four or five feet from the entrance when a huge, tawny-coloured wolf came barrelling out, almost knocking her down. Hot on its heels came a stream of eight pups. My footsteps on top of the hummock had apparently startled the adult wolf inside. I dashed back to the lip of the hummock to see Lia standing below me with a mass of wolf pups milling around her legs. All she had to do was reach down and pick one up.

The rest of the pups soon scampered back into the den, but I managed to catch another before it disappeared inside. Despite their age of some seven weeks, both pups were submissive and everyone took advantage of the opportunity to hold the little fellows and to have their pictures taken. We soon returned the pups to their den and quickly headed back to camp to avoid disturbing the wolves any further. The white wolf escorted us halfway back.

Although most visits to wolf dens don't produce as much excitement as this one did, my clients and I have had many experiences similar to this over the years. I've walked up to active wolf dens hundreds of times, but apart from having wolves howl or bark at me, I've never been threatened in any way. I have yet to hear a wolf growl or to see one bare its teeth. I have watched wolves actively defend their young against such formidable predators as grizzlies, but when it comes to humans they don't even try.

To illustrate how intimidated wolves can be of people, even when their pups are clearly at risk, another incident on the Thelon River comes to mind. Our canoeing party had just investigated an active den without seeing any wolves. As we were about to leave, I looked back towards the den and saw a big white male wolf standing in plain view carrying a good-sized pup in his mouth. The wolf was holding the pup by one hind leg and pup's head was almost dragging on the ground. Without really thinking about it, I charged the wolf. The big male stood his ground as I ran straight at him as fast as I could. I knew he would eventually cave in, but it wasn't until I was about ten feet from him that he finally dropped the pup and ran. I soon caught the pup, but the big white wolf disappeared and we never saw him again.

My clients and I have probably had more thrilling experiences with tundra wolves than with all other species of arctic wildlife combined. The wolf is the animal my clients most want to see, and a lot of people have joined my trips for that reason alone. While nothing is guaranteed, it's a rare trip indeed when we fail to encounter wolves. In fact, some trips have produced sightings of as many as twenty or thirty of these beautiful, big predators. But important as this animal has been to the success of my business, the wolf has had an even greater influence on the course of my life. After all, it was the wolf that originally led me to the Arctic and my profession of these past several decades. The wolf even played a role in my marriage, but that's a story in its own right that I think I'll save for later.

The Big Black Ox

Muskoxen may seem docile enough, but the bulls are formidable animals that will stand their ground against all challengers, including man. We've had a few frightening encounters with muskoxen over the years, some more serious than others. One of these incidents involved two women clients of mine on a warm, still night on the Thelon River. These two women had pitched their tent near mine and had opened up the tent's nylon doors at both ends to allow the air to flow through. There was nothing between them and the great outdoors but two big panels of insect netting.

In the twilight of two o'clock in the morning I was suddenly awakened by the women screaming, followed by the rumble of heavy hooves. A big bull muskox had walked up to their tent and had pushed his nose up against the insect netting, just inches from their heads while they slept. After the muskox had filled his nostrils with the scent of the occupants inside, he had become alarmed and had let out a terrific snort which, of course, had jolted the women out of their sleep.

Another time, a whole herd of muskoxen wandered in amongst our tents at night. Again, they were probably alarmed by the strange scent of humans. They stampeded. I was rudely awakened by snorts and thundering hooves, but there was nothing I could do but cringe as the entire herd crashed through the dwarf birch bushes beside my tent and raced by on both sides of me only a few feet away. For a few seconds I was convinced I was going to be trampled to death. Amazingly, not a single guy line on any of our tents was touched in the stampede.

A lot of our muskox sightings in the Barren Lands are of unattached bulls. In the summer, bull muskoxen are continually being displaced from the herds by more dominant males. The bulls are usually sighted as singles or in pairs, but small groups of up to six or seven males are sometimes encountered. Unlike the muskoxen of the High Arctic Islands, mainland animals are very large beasts. Bulls can weigh close to one thousand pounds.

Bull muskoxen are easily approachable. Indeed, it's easy to get *too* close, which can be dangerous. Sometimes they'll charge. If you know what kinds of behaviour to look for, they'll usually warn you when they want you to back off.

On one of my very first canoe trips in the Barren Lands I approached a bull muskox too closely. If he gave me any warning signs that he was getting uncomfortable, I didn't recognize them. All I remember was looking at this big fellow through the telephoto lens of my camera when suddenly he was coming at me full bore. It happened so fast that by the time I dropped the camera, the infuriated charging monster was no more than ten or fifteen feet away. It looked like I had only a second or two left to live.

At that very instant, the big bull's front legs buckled from under him and he fell flat on his face at my very feet. I turned and ran for my life! After I'd run some distance I looked back. The muskox was standing where he had fallen, glowering at me.

The ground where that bull muskox fell was as level and smooth as a Winnipeg front lawn. I have no rational explanation for what happened to that muskox. But maybe, just maybe, I had experienced a miracle.

Encounters with Grizzlies

Of all the large mammals on the tundra, the grizzly and the wolverine seem to be the most fearful of man. This is surprising in the case of the grizzly, because on the Barrens the grizzly is king, and I'm certain that very few of these bears have ever encountered humans. Regardless, most grizzlies that pick up your scent a mile downwind will run off as fast as they can. There are always exceptions, of course; grizzlies are notoriously unpredictable.

One of the most intimidating things about grizzlies is what they nearly always do when they first become aware of you: stand up on their hind legs. When they drop down on all fours again, you're always left wondering which way they're going to go—at you or away from you. Nevertheless, after decades of encounters with grizzlies, the only truly aggressive bears that have confronted my clients and me have been a few sows with cubs that we approached too closely in our canoes. I've never carried firearms on any of my guided trips and I've never regretted that decision. That doesn't mean we haven't had a few frightening experiences with grizzlies over the years. But our lives have never been endangered.

One time, a huge blond bear ran up to within twenty-five feet of one of my clients on the tundra. Although she was terrified, she managed to suppress her natural impulse to flee and the grizzly finally ran off. It turned out the bear was just curious but, of course, it was a near heart-stopping experience for my client.

One of my very first encounters with a grizzly, and one that gave me reason to develop a healthier respect for the unpredictability of the grizzly bear's temperament, involved a bear that walked into our camp one evening on the Coppermine River. My clients were in bed and I had just finished my chores when I noticed the grizzly walking down the shore towards me. I certainly didn't want a bear hanging around my food and equipment at night so I decided the appropriate thing to do was to put the fear of the Lord into that bear so he'd never come back. Scooping up two frying pans, I marched up to him, scolding him loudly and beating the pans together. Back in those days I was probably no more afraid of grizzlies than I was of black bears, of which I had no fear at all.

The grizzly's reaction to my aggressive advance was to retreat, but just a little. Much to my surprise, he did not run away. Time and again he would stand his ground and let me get close before he would slowly move off up the shore. We kept this little contest of wills going for nearly an hour. I didn't like the surly look in that bear's eyes and I stayed within a few feet of the river at all times. It was deep and swift right to the shore, providing me with an avenue of escape. I managed to move the grizzly almost a mile up the river before I finally left him and returned to camp. It was an unnerving experience and one I will never forget.

I've always been of the opinion that water would be the best means of escape from an aggressive bear. I've watched grizzlies swim a number of times, and I've never been impressed by their speed. Diving and swimming long distances underwater, I think, would be an especially effective way to elude a bear. However, in the summer of 2000, my friends Jay and Carolyn Pritchett witnessed a feat by a swimming grizzly that has given me second thoughts. As Jay and Carolyn watched, a big grizzly chased a bull caribou into the Back River in front of their campsite. The caribou is the mammal I consider to be the fastest swimmer on the tundra, and this particular bull caribou had a fifty-yard head start on the grizzly. Nevertheless, the bear caught and killed the caribou before it had gone more than a few hundred yards across the river. Jay told me it was the most formidable display of speed and raw power he'd ever seen in his life.

The strength of the grizzly is indeed incredible. It's a common sight in the Barren Lands to see parts of hillsides that have been torn up by these bears in their attempts to unearth ground squirrels. Sometimes it looks as if a bulldozer has been at work. One wonders, however, about the energy expended by the grizzly in this task versus the energy gained by a mouthful of ground squirrel. Once, as we ate breakfast, we watched a rather small, unimpressive-looking grizzly dig up a ground squirrel from under a pile of boulders, no more than two hundred yards from where we stood. The boulders were big; most men would have had difficulty lifting even the smallest of them. Yet that grizzly tossed them into the air as if they were ping-pong balls.

In the fall, the grizzly puts its prodigious strength and digging abilities to good use by excavating a den, where it sleeps away the worst of the winter. Over the years, I've come across a number of these dens, most of them on eskers. All have been in sandy locations, either on a steep south-facing slope or on a vertical cut-bank where the snow would drift over the entrance. All of the dens I have located were dug down on an angle for six or eight feet, with a slight enlargement at the bottom that served as the sleeping chamber. One was a wolf den that had been enlarged.

Barren-ground grizzlies emerge from their dens in April or May, before winter has fully released its grip on the tundra. Aboriginal people along the western Arctic Coast report that grizzlies are often attached to muskox herds at this time of the year—the same months that muskoxen are giving birth to their calves. Newborn muskox calves may be subjected to heavy predation by grizzlies in the Barren Lands, especially in those parts where grizzlies are relatively abundant. I have often wondered what impact grizzly predation has on muskox populations. Grizzly predation could neatly explain the recent crash in muskox numbers along the middle Thelon River and more northern parts of the Barren Lands.

During the summer, I have often come upon grizzlies asleep beside muskoxen they have killed. Usually, these kills have been large bulls. Grizzlies are probably most successful in catching single bull muskoxen that are sleeping or feeding in dense willow thickets, but even out on the open tundra, sleeping bulls are vulnerable to attack. I have often awakened muskoxen by getting close enough to bounce pebbles off them. I even kicked a few in the rear end when I was younger and more foolish.

On the last day of my season in 1997 one of these sleeping grizzlies gave me a few frightening moments. I was about to begin preparing our final supper when I noticed some ravens circling a nearby hilltop. Suspecting a wolf kill, I grabbed my video camera and went for a look. I had just climbed the last little knoll up on top of the hill when I noticed something dark lying on a patch of sand thirty yards in front of me. It was a grizzly, and he was sound asleep, facing away from me. The bear was upwind of me and the wind was blowing strongly, muffling any sounds. It turned out he had a freshly killed caribou a short distance away.

Holding my camera and looking at a dozing grizzly, literally an easy stone's throw away, I asked myself, "Do I get the hell out of here or do I take some great video?" I decided to take some great video. I raised the camera and flipped the little latch to turn it on. Incredibly, the sleeping bear appeared to hear the click of the latch above the noise of the wind. He raised his head and looked around, but I was behind him and he never looked my way. He seemed to be satisfied all was well and put his head down again to sleep. After shooting some film, I flipped the camera latch off. The bear had indeed heard that sound because he raised his head once more. This time he got up. That was enough for me. I was getting out of there.

I backed down the knoll and was still backing up on the open tundra when the grizzly appeared on top of the knoll thirty yards away, right where I had stood. Grizzlies have poor eyesight so I stood rock still. Since the bear didn't look at me, I assumed he hadn't spotted me, even though I was directly in front of him, in plain view. Or had he? Now he was walking straight towards me. I continued to film all this. However, when the grizzly started walking up to me, I quickly lost my nerve. I dropped the camera and raised both arms. I was about to shout, but the bear had already spun around and was starting to run away. But for a few moments there I had that sinking feeling you get just before panic sets in.

The most frightening thing that has ever happened to me in the Barren Lands was an encounter with a grizzly near Ursus Islands on the Thelon River in 1986. My clients and I had decided to take a day off from paddling and go for a long walk. Six of us canoed a mile or two across a lake-like widening in the river to climb a big tundra hill, while Lia and two others stayed in camp. Throughout my guiding career, there has always been an abundance of bears in the Ursus Islands area, so I asked Lia to stay in camp to guard our belongings from any grizzly that might happen by.

The hill we had chosen for our hike was five hundred feet high and several miles across. About noon, we reached the top of one of the highest ridges, where we ate our lunch overlooking a great sweep of tundra. As we were soon to discover, the top of that hill was a little wildlife paradise. After lunch we wandered around, photographing rough-legged hawks, peregrine falcons, sandhill cranes, scattered caribou and a few small bunches of muskoxen. We had begun to circle back towards our canoes when I noticed a good-sized grizzly five hundred yards away, in the exact spot where we had eaten our lunch. Since we were downwind, I thought if we stayed out of sight we could outflank the bear while heading back in the direction of our canoes. The grizzly appeared to be going the opposite way, and I believed that if we got off the top of the hill without being seen he would never even know we had been there.

My strategy appeared to be working at first. We were two or three miles away from our canoes with over a mile to go before we would start our final descent. We were walking fast and I kept looking back to see if the grizzly was in sight. When we reached the bottom of a big saddle, still high above our canoes, I looked back and saw the grizzly running flat out in our direction, right on our trail. Although the bear was still a mile away, he was coming so fast that I knew we only had a few minutes before he would catch up to us. At this point, I could only hope the direction the grizzly was running in was purely coincidental. However, it certainly looked as if he was tracking us by scent. I was beginning to get very frightened about the idea of a grizzly overtaking us on the open tundra at high speed.

When we were climbing the hill before lunch we had come upon a large pond on top of the first ridge. From where we now stood we couldn't see the pond, but I thought it was nearby. We turned ninety degrees into the wind from our previous direction of travel to head for where I thought the pond was. One of the women in our group was unable to run, so we had to settle for a fast walk. Luckily, the pond was even closer than I thought and we reached it with seconds to spare. I told the others to wait at the water's edge while I peeked over the top of the slope leading down to the pond to keep an eye on the grizzly. If the bear was still on our trail after our ninety-degree turn, I knew our troubles were just beginning.

The first rule when meeting up with a grizzly is don't run; stand your ground and face the bear. However, I was positive that up to that point, this animal had not seen us. If he was following us, it was by scent.

There he was.

I'm sure my adrenaline was flowing and my heart was pounding as I watched that grizzly close in on the place where we had made our ninety-degree turn. He was running so fast when he hit the turn that he overshot by some fifty yards. Without breaking stride, he wheeled on an arc until he was back on our track, coming right at me. Any faint hope I still had that this bear wasn't tracking us now evaporated.

Close to panic now, I ran down the slope to the pond and ordered everyone into the water. No one hesitated for even a second. The pond was a substantial one, shallow near shore and warm from the long days of intense sunshine. Everyone ran into the water—cameras, binoculars and all. I dropped my camera and binoculars on shore and was last to wade in. We were all standing chest to neck deep in the pond within twenty or thirty yards of shore when the grizzly raced into sight and headed straight for us.

The bear ran full speed right to the water's edge, then suddenly braked to a stop. We were all yelling and splashing water at this point, hoping to frighten him. The grizzly just stood there staring at us, his face streaked with foamy, white saliva from his long, hard run. After a few minutes, he looked away and began to shuffle about on the shore, peering this way and that, but never directly at us. He seemed to be ignoring us completely.

When I was convinced the bear wasn't coming into the pond after us, I suggested to Charlie, who was standing next to me, that he take a photograph. It was a wonderful opportunity. Charlie was standing neck deep in the water holding his camera on top of his head. This was one of the few cameras that had survived our watery retreat. With an earnest look on his face, Charlie whispered to me that he thought he'd better not. He was afraid the sound of the camera shutter might annoy the bear.

Finally, casually, the bear wandered off. For whatever reason, we were no longer of interest. After another five or ten minutes, I sneaked out of the pond for a look. The grizzly was nowhere in sight.

We got down off the hill as fast as we could, and we didn't relax until we were in our canoes. I vowed I would never climb that hill again until I was certain that bear had died of old age. Looking back on it now, I'm convinced the grizzly was simply extremely curious. Once he caught up to us, he never did anything that could be considered aggressive. Most grizzlies are repelled by human scent; this one was apparently attracted by it. Even if the grizzly had caught up to us on the open tundra, I'm pretty certain we would have been safe. But I'm still grateful that pond was there.

By the time we got back to camp it was evident that two people had been badly shaken by the experience. The effects lasted for another few days. One fellow was hoarse for the rest of the trip from shouting at the bear. Although the rest of us had been frightened, we were fine once we were safe back in camp.

One member of the group chased into the pond was Stu Mackinnon. Stu joins one of my trips every year. He's not a strong swimmer, and you hardly ever see him without his life jacket on. He even takes it to bed with him to use as a pillow. When we hiked up the hill that day, Stu had left his life jacket in the canoe. After we returned to camp, Stu told me, with his typical dry sense of humour, that in the future, he supposed, he'd better wear his life jacket on our hikes as well. When I asked him if he had been frightened by the grizzly, Stu replied: "Not really; after all, you were there." When I asked him what he meant by that, he said he was confident that at the appropriate moment I would have sacrificed myself to the bear in order to save the lives of my clients. What I didn't tell Stu was that when I jumped into that pond I was confident I could outswim the bear, or at least Stu Mackinnon.

Ravenous

Any good-sized northern community is home to hundreds of big, brazen ravens that scavenge for garbage or unattended food wherever they can find it. Beyond the communities, ravens are thinly scattered and very shy of humans. Throughout the winter, many of these rural birds follow the caribou migrations, where scavenging on wolf kills provides a major source of food. By spring, ravens are widely dispersed at nesting sites raising their young.

It was therefore a surprise when Dennis Voigt and I began to see large flocks of ravens in June of 1973 as we paddled out onto remote White Wolf Lake, just north of treeline. These ravens, we soon discovered, were feasting on large numbers of skinned-out carcasses of wolves and wolverines floating in the lake and littering the shorelines. We later found out this was the home base of Fred Riddle, one of the very last of the old barrenland trappers. During the "caribou crisis" of the 1950s, Riddle was one of a handful of white trappers contracted by the federal government to poison wolves with strychnine. After the poisoning campaign ended, though, Riddle continued to illegally poison the tundra wolves that migrated with the caribou herds into his area during the winter. He was finally charged with this offence in 1974, brought to trial in Fort Smith and fined a paltry seventy-five dollars. From the early 1950s until he was fined in 1974, Riddle poisoned between two hundred and four hundred wolves every winter for their pelts. The vicinity of Fred Riddle's camp on White Wolf Lake probably supported as many ravens on a year-round basis as any medium sized town in the Northwest Territories.

As any northerner will tell you, ravens are not only highly social, but very intelligent. As an extension of the age-old relationship between ravens and wolves in the wild, urban ravens have a particular fondness, it seems, for ganging up on dogs in order to steal their food. Once, I watched a group of ravens use their considerable intelligence and some amazing teamwork to outwit a dog guarding an animal carcass near my home in Fort Smith. The dog was tethered on a long chain to a kennel and the carcass it was feeding on was lying in the dirt nearby.

Four or five ravens were fanned out in a semicircle on the ground beyond the carcass and out of reach of the dog. One of the ravens then challenged the dog by hopping up to the carcass and taking a peck at it. This brought the dog charging out of its kennel in an attempt to kill the raven. The raven reacted by hopping almost nonchalantly back out of reach of the dog. The raven knew precisely where the chain would stop the dog, but the dog, it seemed, didn't. When it reached the end of its chain, still running flat out, the poor beast was snapped to a near neck-breaking halt, just a foot or two short of the raven. Meanwhile, another raven had quickly hopped in to snatch a tasty morsel off the carcass before the dog realized it was there. When the dog ran after the second raven, it too hopped just beyond the length of the chain, and the dog was slammed to a stop again, just short of the raven.

The ravens continued to take turns at luring the dog off in one direction while another bird or two would hop in from another angle for a few pecks at the carcass. In the process, the ravens were driving the dog into a frenzy. The dim-witted dog never did figure out that the way to stop the depredation was to simply stay with the carcass. As a result, the ravens had some sport and got fed, as well. Pretty smart birds, those ravens.

Power over Grizzlies

When sixteen-year-old Jonah Kelly joined one of my trips, he wanted to see a grizzly more than anything else in the world. I cautioned him that it was a bit of a long shot. The central Barrens may be the best place in North America to see caribou and wolves, but that certainly isn't the case for grizzlies. One can easily go on several of my trips without seeing a bear, and sometimes I see no more than one or two over the course of a summer. But Jonah was obsessed with grizzlies; he just knew he was going to be lucky.

When we made our last camp of the trip near Thelon Bluffs, the closest we had come to a grizzly was spotting some tracks in the sand along the river. It was a hot afternoon, and the only thing the rest of us had on our minds was lying in the river to escape the heat. However, Jonah still hadn't given up on seeing a bear. He told me he was going to take one last look up in the big tundra hills behind our campsite.

I was floating in the river when I saw Jonah returning to camp. He was walking fast, almost dancing. I could tell he was excited from a half mile away, and I guessed he'd finally seen his bear. By the time he reached me at the river, Jonah was practically jumping up and down. Half an hour earlier he had run into a sow with three tiny cubs—his very first grizzlies. Like most bears, they were more afraid of him than he was of them. They had fled, but not before Jonah had had a good look at them. I was happy for Jonah. I knew this was something he'd never forget as long as he lived.

The next summer, Jonah joined another of my trips, convinced he was going to see more grizzlies. One night early in the trip, I heard a few whoops. Jonah was coming down the hill behind camp after one of his evening hikes, elated because he'd seen another bear.

Within the next three days we saw *four* more grizzlies. One evening, two of my clients, who were returning from a hike, surprised a huge bear, which ran full tilt right through our campsite within ten or twenty feet of some of our tents. Then we came upon another two grizzlies feasting on a muskox carcass, and spent an hour in our canoes with a young bear that was as approachable as if it had been behind bars in a zoo. It even followed us down the river when we left. That trip set a new record for the number of grizzlies seen.

In my bones I know we owed all of those grizzlies to Jonah. Experienced hunters will know what I'm talking about. Some hunters seem to have all of the luck and bag most of the game. You can make those animals appear through sheer power of positive thinking. If you believe you'll see bears, those bears will materialize. In any event, Jonah holds the record for grizzlies on my trips with nine encountered in twenty-two days.

Another kind of mental power over bears may arise from feelings that are the exact opposite of Jonah's. Anne had a great fear of bears. I told her what I had told Jonah, that encounters with bears were unlikely. In fact, in this case the chances were highly remote because we were in the southern Barrens on the edge of the range of both black bears and grizzlies.

On the last morning of the trip, a clear, quiet mid-August day, the peace of our camp was suddenly shattered by the most blood-curdling scream I had ever heard. Someone was running down the slope of the esker we were camped on screaming for her very life. I took off instantly to see what was wrong.

It was Anne, and she had just met a bear. She was very agitated, but uninjured. Some other members of our party were up on the esker with their binoculars by now and they reported a grizzly running flat out on the tundra, heading in the opposite direction as fast as it could go.

What had happened was that while Anne was climbing up the long, steep esker on one side, the bear was coming up the other. They reached the top at precisely the same moment, forty feet apart. Anne screamed, the bear panicked, and both turned and fled. However, when I later examined the place where they had met, I had to conclude that Anne had frightened the bear a lot more than it had frightened her. What I found was a long line of liquid blueberries descending the bear's side of the esker: Anne had literally scared the crap out of that bear.

The Elusive Wolverine

The wolverine is one of our largest weasels, and like all members of the weasel family it's high-strung. In fact, I find it difficult to imagine a wolverine sleeping. To me, this animal seems to be little more than a bundle of nerves, always on the go. The wolverine has a distinctive lope that's recognizable even a mile away. Indeed, that's usually how you'll spot a wolverine—off in the distance, running away from you in that steady but peculiar, bounding gait.

Like the wolves, foxes and ravens of the Barren Lands, the wolverine follows the migrating caribou herds in winter, when its main source of food is whatever it can scavenge from wolf kills. Otherwise, the wolverine is omnivorous. For an animal credited with such prodigious strength and ferocity, the wolverine is surprisingly small. Most adults weigh less than forty pounds, and many less than thirty. The wolverine's tracks look like a cross between a wolf's and a bear's, but smaller than either. Its fur is usually dark brown with two broad buff-coloured stripes running along its flanks. In the Barren Lands, these stripes are often bleached to a creamy white. Once, I saw a wolverine whose stripes were so dominant that the whole animal was almost white.

Like nearly all mammals in the Barren Lands, the wolverine is a good swimmer. In the summer of 2001, when we were lining our canoes down a heavy rapid, a wolverine came loping along the far shore of the river. When it spotted us, it stopped and stared, then jumped in the river and started swimming towards us. About halfway across, after disappearing several times in the big waves and holes, it changed its mind and retreated to the far shore. This was one of the few times I've been in a position to form an opinion on the wolverine's intelligence. So far, I haven't been impressed.

The wolverine is the most difficult animal to see on the tundra. I used to say that you can only expect to see one wolverine for every ten grizzlies or hundred wolves encountered. However, I've seen far more wolverines in the past decade than in the previous two combined; now, I see as many of them as I do grizzlies. Still, the wolverine is an elusive animal. Without consulting my diaries I would guess I've seen fewer than fifty over the past thirty years. I've had more luck seeing them in the Back River area than anywhere else. We see between two and five wolverines on every canoe trip there.

Once, I found a wolverine that appeared to have died under unusual circumstances. It was lying, with a wound in its side, at the base of a spruce tree that held an active eagle's nest. The wolverine must have met its demise when it climbed the tree to snack on the young eaglets in their nest. Perhaps the adult birds had attacked, but for whatever reason, the wolverine had evidently fallen out of the tree and had fatally speared itself on a dead snag on the way down.

Because wolverines are extremely wary of humans, most of my sightings have been little more than fleeting glimpses. Nevertheless, I have been close to wolverines on a number of occasions. Once, when I was videotaping a caribou, I noticed its attention was on something between us and to my left. While continuing to film the caribou, I shifted my gaze to the caribou's point of interest and there, standing right out in the open, not more than thirty feet from me, was a wolverine. As I turned the camera on it, the big weasel stared at me for several seconds, then ran up past the caribou. The caribou just stood there and watched the wolverine run by, not ten feet away. I watched the animal run by several dozen more caribou, which also failed to react to it.

On another occasion, I was sitting beside our canoes pulled up on shore, while my clients were fishing a rapid for grayling a short distance away. Hearing some splashing in the little bay behind me, I looked around to see a wolverine loping along the shoreline towards me. When we met, just a few feet apart, the wolverine fled, followed by me in hot pursuit. I soon chased it under a big rock, where it snarled and hissed at me. Since I didn't have my camera, I decided to take a chance and retrieve it from my canoe; but by the time I returned to the big rock, the wolverine was disappearing over a nearby hill.

The wolverine is probably the best index of the health of the wilderness that we have. A thinly spread species in even the best of habitats, it avoids most aspects of human intrusion and civilization. When people invade its wilderness domain, the wolverine usually moves out. Once found throughout almost all of Canada and much of the northern half of the United States, the wolverine is now almost extinct in southern and eastern Canada and in the United States south of Alaska. Not surprisingly, its last centres of relative abundance are in British Columbia, Alaska, Yukon, the Northwest Territories and Nunavut.

Treed

One June, I had several fun-loving guys in their twenties and thirties on one of my canoe trips. Every evening until about eleven, they liked to get together in Rick's tent to play a little poker and have a few drinks and some laughs. Around ten o'clock one night, I was just straightening up some things in the camp kitchen before heading off to bed when some movement caught my eye back in the trees. We were well south of treeline, but the big white spruce trees were widely scattered on a carpet of lichen with no underbrush. About a hundred yards away I saw a black bear strolling along with three tiny cubs no bigger than raccoons. All of my clients were in their tents for the night and from the sound of the chatter and laughter, the poker game in Rick's tent seemed to be in full swing. The bears were minding their own business, and I judged, from the direction they were going in that they'd pass well behind our camp. I watched them disappear from view and was confident I would never see them again.

As it turned out, though, the bears changed direction just after I lost sight of them. Rick and two other fellows were engrossed in having a good time when they heard some strange-sounding vocalizations, and branches breaking on the big spruce tree just a few feet outside the door of their tent. Rick figured it was one of the other guys, so he yelled out to him to quit fooling around and to come on in for a drink and a round of poker. However, there was no reply, and the branches on the spruce tree continued to snap. Some of them were even falling on the top of the tent. Rick muttered, "What the hell?" and went out for a look.

The bears must have walked right up to Rick's tent, and only then become alarmed by the noise. The sow had sent the three little cubs up the tree beside the tent, then she had followed them herself. When Rick came out of his tent, there were four bears looking down at him from fifteen feet up that spruce tree.

The commotion at Rick's tent soon brought the rest of us out of our beds to gather at the base of the tree. After some of the excitement had died down, I suggested we all back off some distance to give the bears a chance to escape. No sooner had we done so than mama bear quickly backed down the tree, followed by the three cubs, who were as agile as monkeys. They lost little time in getting out of there, and we never saw them again. We all returned to our tents, and the poker players retired for a nightcap and a few final hands of cards.

My Bear Alarm

The only thing I ever worry about on my canoe trips is a bear coming into our camp at night while we're asleep and destroying our food and equipment. Fortunately, the chances of that happening are remote compared to places farther south where bears have become conditioned to associate people with food. In the areas where we travel, very few bears ever encounter human beings. When they do, their most common reaction is avoidance.

Nevertheless, bears do walk into our campsites on occasion. The difference between these bears and the ones living closer to civilization is that the bear that wanders into our campsite is probably not there searching for food. It's just passing through. The key is never to give that bear an excuse to linger. He has one of the keenest noses on the planet, so you can never afford to have any food odours associated with your campsite. The worst offence is fish guts. Fish guts will attract bears that are miles downwind.

One precaution I take is to forbid my clients to put fish in their canoes. I once had a black bear chew a hole in a Royalex canoe where a lake trout had slapped its tail against it over twenty-four hours earlier. Another precaution I take is to put my food inside so many layers of plastic bags that my food packs are completely odourless, even to bears. As proof of this, I have seen the tracks of grizzlies that walked right by my packs in the night without disturbing them. The one chink in my armour is my bag of garbage, but I learned how to use that smell to my advantage a long time ago.

Sometime in the early 1980s I realized I couldn't expect my good fortune to protect my food packs from bears forever. About four o'clock one morning, a large black bear demolished my garbage bag and most of a sack of freeze-dried food before it awoke me. The garbage was double-bagged in plastic, but it was far from airtight. Obviously, it had acted as a magnet for that bear once the animal had entered our camp.

I decided that if I was ever going to sleep soundly at night again, I'd have to develop a device to frighten bears away from my kitchen, or at least warn me of their presence there. Since the garbage was the most attractive thing in our camp to bears, the solution was to attach this device to the garbage bag. That way, I would be warned of the bear before it could damage anything of value.

My initial idea was to take a can of insect killer sealed under pressure, coat it with honey and place it beside my garbage bag at night. If a bear bit into the pressurized can it would explode in the animal's mouth, driving it off. However, one of my clients, who was much more mechanically gifted than I, soon came up with a much better idea. He rigged up a five-dollar, battery-powered window alarm inside an empty jam can and tied the can to my garbage bag. The opening on the can and the release mechanism on the alarm were covered with an aluminium pie plate, and the whole thing was held down with a flat rock. What's more, the contraption was rain-proof. Any bear that grabbed the garbage would upset the can, triggering the alarm. One of the weaknesses of those cheap little alarms, though, is that they aren't loud enough to wake me unless my tent is pitched close to my kitchen. That's not a problem except during the height of the bug season, when my kitchens are out on rock bars, some distance from where I'm able to place my tent.

Only once has my bear alarm ever gone off. It was one night on the Thelon River during the blackfly season, and my tent was a long way off. Although I didn't hear the alarm myself, my old friend Bob Hawkings in the tent next to mine did. Bob woke me up, and I quickly went down to the kitchen to investigate. The garbage bag had been torn open all right, but there was no animal in sight. The next morning we found the fresh tracks of a fox in the sand. The alarm had probably frightened it off before Bob had alerted me. Even though my only experience with a marauding bear was that one black bear incident those many years ago, I still connect my bear alarm to the garbage bag every night before I go to bed. It gives me peace of mind, and I know I sleep better.

Underfoot

About ten o'clock one evening in late July I was down at the edge of the Thelon River, washing up before retiring for the night. My clients were already in their tents on top of a high bank behind me, overlooking the river. As I brushed my teeth I faced the sun, now low in the sky directly across the river. The sun was so bright glaring off the water that it was almost impossible to see anything in that general direction.

Just then, the tranquillity of the evening was interrupted by what sounded like the grunting and honking of large numbers of caribou. I shielded my eyes with my hand and squinted into the sun towards the far side of the Thelon. The river was bristling with antlers; a large mass of caribou was swimming across, and they were going to come ashore right where I was standing. I dropped everything and ran up to my clients' tents to warn them that our campsite was about to be invaded.

For the next hour we all stood on the edge of the riverbank and photographed caribou coming ashore and streaming by our tents. In all, about twenty thousand animals passed through.

When the last stragglers had disappeared, I remembered I had dropped my towel on the stones near the water's edge. Since a large part of the herd had come ashore at that very spot, I expected it to be trampled beyond recognition. I went down to investigate, and to my surprise it was lying exactly as I had left it. Although thousands of hooves had passed within inches of it, all of those caribou had evidently recognized that towel as some kind of foreign object and not one of them had stepped on it.

Winter Journey on the Barrens

Only once have I ever been to the Barren Lands in winter. In the mid-1980s my friend Cormack Gates, a biologist, invited me to help him conduct some "recruitment counts" on caribou herds to determine what percentage of calves had survived the winter, as an index of potential population growth.

In early March, Cormack and I flew to the upper Hanbury River from Fort Smith in a Single Otter ski plane with snowmobiles, toboggans, a wall tent and full winter gear. The caribou biologist from Yellowknife was already there. According to him, most of the Bathurst and Beverly caribou herds were together on the upper Hanbury at the time. There were certainly a lot of caribou. Aggregations of many thousands were scattered about a relatively small area.

Cormack had spent the previous several years as the regional biologist for the Keewatin District, stationed in Rankin Inlet on Hudson Bay. There, he had travelled extensively with the Inuit and was familiar with their winter travel techniques.

Snow in the Barrens becomes hard-packed from the wind and is easily traversed by man and beast alike. However, it also made the terrain totally unrecognizable to me, despite the fact that we were in an area I knew well. I was like a duck out of water. With the white glare of the snow everywhere, I found it hard to tell the lakes from the tundra. Fortunately, Lia had given me her heavy-duty mountaineering sunglasses with leather side-flaps. Without them, I wouldn't have been able to see a thing. Topographical features were so difficult to distinguish that one day I drove my snowmobile over a cliff. I didn't even realize I'd done so until I felt myself floating free of the machine. My greatest fear was being hit by the fully loaded toboggan I was pulling behind. By sheer luck, everything—me included—landed right side up and uninjured below.

Cormack and I classified thousands of caribou every day. The procedure for doing this involved Cormack peering through a high-powered spotting scope at caribou rectums. Since all of the mature bulls had dropped their antlers, they were difficult to distinguish from the antlerless cows until Cormack examined their rear ends. For hours at a time, Cormack would call out the different classes of animals—cow, calf, big bull, young bull—and I would dutifully pencil them down.

The most interesting part of this whole experience for both of us was the wolves. There must have been thousands of them. The caribou biologist thought that most of the caribou in the Bathurst and Beverly herds were in the area, and most of the tundra wolves attached to these two herds were undoubtedly present as well. There was hardly a minute, day or night, when we couldn't hear them howling. The visibility remained poor, but we could sometimes make out little groups of wolves scattered about on hilltops.

It's my belief that the wolf packs were constantly howling to warn the others to keep clear. What they were saying in effect was "We're here; stay away from us." With so many wolves crammed into such a small area, along with hundreds of thousands of their prey, they had

A three-to-four-week-old tundra wolf pup.

Highly mobile wolf pups at a rendezvous site on an island in the Thelon River.

An esker west of the Thelon Wildlife Sanctuary. Note the spruce trees sheltered on the south side of the esker. Eskers are the inverted beds of long-dead rivers that flowed under the melting glaciers some 9,000 years ago.

A double rainbow, mid-August, upper Thelon River.

Bull caribou (part of the Beverly herd) near treeline in mid-August. Note that their antlers are still covered in velvet and their white manes are beginning to develop.

A grizzly asleep beside his partially-eaten kill of a bull muskox on the shore of the Thelon River.

A curious barren-ground grizzly approaches the photographer, Back River, Thelon Wildlife Sanctuary.
PHOTO BY NORMA HAMILTON.

Wilberforce Falls, Hood River near Bathurst Inlet. This 165-foot falls is the highest in the Barren Lands.

This curious young grizzly on a beach on the Thelon River showed neither aggression nor fear when approached by our five canoes.
PHOTO BY PETER ALBRECHT.

"Garnet Falls" on a small creek in the Thelon Oasis. In this little spot, there are columbine, raspberries and currants, hundreds of miles north of where you'd expect to find them.

The edge of the Barrens. The setting sun has broken through black clouds just above the horizon, bathing the land in an eerie golden light.

Our canoes on the upper Thelon River looking across at a sand dune.

Sunset, late August, south of the treeline.

to stay vocal in order to keep their packs separated. One day we saw twenty-one wolves, more than Cormack had seen in his entire four years as a biologist in the Keewatin.

It was a unique experience, but the lasting impression I have after all these years, despite the huge numbers of caribou, is the desolation of the Barren Lands in winter. Everything was white—the ground, the lakes and the sky. It was the bleakest place I've ever seen in my life.

PART IV

Memorable Characters

A Most Remarkable Client

I've met many remarkable people through my guiding service, but George Thompson was unique. George was a forty-eight-year-old blind schoolteacher from Portland, Oregon, who joined one of my canoe trips in 1995, along with his wife, Margot, and several of their friends. He had lost his sight from diabetes at the age of twenty-seven.

George's exuberance and joy in life would have been remarkable in anyone, blind or sighted. He was a virtuoso on the mandolin, had a fine voice and belonged to a folk-singing group. He entertained us on many evenings, leading us in sing-songs around the campfire. I sometimes accompanied him on the mouth organ.

George did everything we did. With Margot in the stern of their canoe, George paddled bow. He portaged some of our heaviest packs, and once he even carried a canoe. As we paddled along, Margot kept up a steady description of the landscape and wildlife on both sides of the river for George. Margot got into the finest of details with her descriptions. George would often excitedly ask her questions about what she was seeing, followed by lots of "wows." Occasionally, one of their friends would take over for Margot to give her a break.

In rapids, Margot would tell George when to draw left or right and how forcefully. Crossing portages or going on hikes, Margot would walk several feet in front of George. George would hold one end of his walking stick, while Margot held the other end on top of her shoulder. George could anticipate the ups and downs in the footing by feeling the walking stick bobbing up and down on Margot's shoulder. I never saw him fall once during our twelve-day trip.

The highlights of the trip for George, of course, were the sounds. George's favourites were the cries of peregrine falcons as we paddled by their aerie, the thudding hooves of a caribou as it passed within a few feet of his tent and the howls of several wolves that the rest of us watched at our last camp. George was easily the most verbally appreciative and cheerful client I have ever had in my guiding career. I found the whole experience uplifting. George's enthusiasm served to remind me how, too often, the rest of us take our good fortune for granted.

Jack

Well over one hundred bush pilots have flown me into and out of the Barren Lands over the years, but Jack Baron was one who stood out by virtue of his competence, intelligence and engaging personality. When Jack began flying out of Fort Smith, he would file his flight plans over the radio, and he became quite intrigued by the seductive voice of the radio operator. The voice belonged to Joanne, and before long she and Jack were married. Their two little boys were about the same age as mine.

In the spring of 1992 Jack borrowed an airplane from his employer and flew his new family down to southern British Columbia, where he and Joanne had been raised (though they didn't meet until they moved to the North). Partway through their visit with Joanne's parents in Trail, Jack decided to fly to Kamloops to look up some of his old pals. He picked a bad day to fly to Kamloops, but thank God he was alone. In the fog, his plane struck a tree on a mountainside, and he was killed.

Jack had been captivated by the Barren Lands when he had flown us in to our canoeing rivers. He had told Joanne that if anything ever happened to him that's where he wanted his ashes to go. So, on July 19, 1992, Joanne gave us a small urn containing her husband's remains, and Jack took his last flight into the Barren Lands. We released his ashes as we swooped in over the Thelon River, then placed the urn in a cairn that we built on a low hill overlooking the river. Every time I paddle by that spot I think of Jack. I think he would be pleased with his final resting place, which to my mind is one of the grandest on the face of this earth.

Billy

Billy Bourque was a big Cree Metis who, with his partner, Dick Funk, built the air charter company I still fly with in Fort Smith. Billy was one of the great bush pilots. As a result of spending too many years flying Single Otters without the benefit of head-phones, Billy was hard of hearing; but he had the eyes of an eagle. He sported a big, black, drooping moustache, and he always wore a big, toothy grin. He reminded me of one of those sly but lovable Mexican banditos you used to see in those old cowboy movies from the 1940s or '50s.

Billy was a terrible tease who got a lot of fun out of life. He was so skilled at kidding that I never knew when I was the victim. He'd land his airplane at a beautiful beach on one of my secret rivers to pick up my canoe party, and remark to me that the place was so beautiful he'd decided to build a fishing cabin on the site. Then he'd burst into guffaws at the worried look on my face and slap his thigh in glee.

In the days before Loran or GPS navigation, a bush pilot had to keep his eyes on the ground and a finger on the map. Since we were always flying over the Canadian Shield, we were constantly above a confusing maze of lakes of every size and shape imaginable; but if you knew the area, you could usually tell where you were by recognizing the major lakes.

We often flew back and forth to our rivers in a fleet of three or four bush planes. When you flew with Billy, you were always well entertained. A lot of our flights lasted a good part of the day, and Billy would be yakking away the whole time—teasing, joking and laughing with his passengers and the other pilots on the two-way radio. About every fifteen minutes, it seemed, he'd ask his pilots where they were and describe his own location. Billy's side of the exchange usually went something like this: "You see that lake up ahead that looks like an upside-down buffalo with a broken front leg? Well, I'm about three miles southwest of that." The other pilots knew the drill. They'd just reply, "Oh yeah," without bothering to try to find which lake Billy was talking about.

One of my favourite Billy Bourque stories dates back to the last day of my guiding season in 1987. It was raining and blowing like hell, but Billy and two of his pilots arrived on time in a Single Otter and two Cessna 185s to return my party to Fort Smith. Since the summer was over, some of the pilots Billy had hired to fly "floats" had already left. That meant he had to call upon Brad, who normally flew the company's aircraft on wheels.

One of my clients on that trip was the recently retired chief pilot for Pan American Airlines. After we tied a canoe onto Brad's Cessna and threw in some packs, the Pan Am pilot got aboard for the trip back to Fort Smith. However, twenty miles short of town, Brad ran out of fuel, and with his engine silenced, he had to glide into a lake below him. It was a good thing Brad didn't run out of fuel five or ten minutes later because the lake he was forced down onto marked the edge of the Canadian Shield, and it was the last substantial piece of water he could come down on before the Slave River at Fort Smith. There was nothing in between but a few beaver ponds.

That day, Billy was flying the other Cessna. As soon as he dropped his load off at the float base in Fort Smith, Billy grabbed some jugs of gas and flew back the twenty miles to rescue Brad. The lake Brad had glided onto was rough and the wind had blown his disabled airplane onto a rocky shore. He had secured the plane in the teeth of the storm as best as he could with ropes, but the waves were still pounding the Cessna's pontoons on the rocks. Billy hoped he could avoid subjecting his airplane to the same kind of punishment, and he saw one possible solution. There was a little, shallow, marshy spot well offshore, but only about a hundred yards from Brad's plane.

When Billy landed, he taxied upwind into the marshy spot and rammed his pontoons into the ooze. There was nothing to tie the airplane to, but with the engine running the Cessna stayed put. When he was convinced his airplane would stay there, Billy stripped down to his underwear and swam over to Brad's plane. Once there, he untied the canoe on the pontoon struts and paddled it back to his own plane to fetch the gas. When he returned to Brad's plane he poured in the fuel, made sure Brad got into the air safely, then paddled the Pan Am pilot back to his own Cessna. With his engine still running, Billy tied on the canoe and then, still naked except for his wet underpants, flew my client back to Fort Smith.

"All in a day's work," declared Billy with his standard big grin and a twinkle in his eye. It was quite a performance, and nobody else could have pulled it off with the same kind of flair and good humour. The Pan Am pilot may not have thought much of Brad's abilities, but he sure was impressed with Billy.

Billy died at the controls of one of his beloved de Havilland Single Otters when the ailerons malfunctioned on a test flight in May, 1993. He left a wife, four children and a lot of others who loved him. He was only forty-four years old. It was a privilege knowing you, Billy.

Mandy

Mandy got off on the wrong foot from the very beginning of her trip with us. When I met my clients at the airport, Mandy was missing, and none of the other trip members had met her anywhere en route. About five minutes after all the other passengers had disembarked, the stewardess helped a feeble-looking old lady down the ramp off the jet. I turned to one of my clients and said, "God, I hope that's not her." It was Mandy, all right!

She didn't bother to greet us when we came over to introduce ourselves. She was too busy complaining about the airlines, which had lost her luggage before she had arrived in Edmonton. One of the merchants in Fort Smith ended up opening her store after hours just for Mandy, and the airline's representative showed up and paid for all of her purchases. Everyone, including me, was trying to be gracious, but Mandy was impossible to please.

As we were soon to discover, out first impressions of Mandy told us a lot about her character. She was a crusty old gal who let you know exactly what was on her mind. And she complained—a lot. She had a particularly icy relationship with a doctor from Wisconsin, who had brought his two teenage grandsons along on the trip. The doctor had made the mistake of saying something nasty about U.S. President Clinton's wife, Hillary. The poor doctor had problems enough without incurring the wrath of Mandy. His grandsons complained continually about the abundance of mosquitoes and the dearth of Cokes and hamburgers.

Mandy had bad feet. She could hardly walk, especially on uneven ground, and she used a walking stick wherever she went. She was a good paddler, though. Nobody else wanted to paddle with her, so she ended up in the bow of my canoe. It didn't take me long to realize that Mandy's bark was worse than her bite. Whenever she started in complaining, I'd just chuckle and say something to make her smile. Another client and I kept on her good side by taking turns carrying her personal pack back and forth between the canoe and her tent.

Mandy shared a tent with Marilyn. Unfortunately for Marilyn, Mandy got up at least three times a night to relieve herself, and when she came back into the tent she brought in hordes of mosquitoes. It was always Marilyn who had to get up to kill them. Mandy's habits—snoring and smoking cigarillos—also failed to ingratiate her with Marilyn. I told Marilyn she could take the spare tent for herself, but she didn't want to insult Mandy. The final straw for Marilyn was one stormy night when Mandy, reluctant to brave the weather, emptied her bladder in the tent's vestibule. To make matters worse, the wind blew some of her bodily fluids back into the tent and onto Marilyn's sleeping bag. The next night Marilyn took the extra tent.

Whenever we hiked off to look at some distant attraction, Mandy insisted on coming along, but her pace was glacial. We frequently had to stop and wait for her to catch up. One morning we walked into a wolf den that lay almost a mile from the river. As usual, Mandy was lagging far behind, but we were on fairly open tundra, so I knew she could see where we had gone.

The den was at the base of a big sand dune, and the last half mile was across bare sand. I had only seen one wolf track in the sand as we approached, and I was sure the den was inactive. There wouldn't be any wolves. I was just going through the motions for my clients. I strolled up to the den, not really paying attention.

Suddenly, two white wolves that had been sleeping on the sand leapt up in front of me and barked. I jumped about a foot off the ground. I had almost stepped on them! The wolves retreated, then posed for a few quick photographs before running off. We spent the next half hour at the den watching and photographing four cute little pups that kept popping in and out of the holes and playing with each other. When Mandy finally caught up to us she was almost beside herself with excitement. The two white wolves that had fled from us had practically knocked her over. She was absolutely thrilled. She talked about it for the rest of the trip.

Near the end of our route we walked in to check out another wolf den behind our camp. This time, Mandy lost sight of us in a clump of trees, got annoyed and turned back. When we returned to camp, Mandy was waiting for me. She really chewed me out for leaving her behind. It was the only time she ever had any harsh words for me, but I could tell she'd forgiven me before long.

A couple of weeks after the trip, a beautiful Patagonia brand vest arrived for me in the mail. It was Mandy's way of saying thank you. Earning her approval was a considerable achievement in my eyes, and I was touched by her gesture of appreciation.

The Last White Trappers

The heyday of the barrenland trapper was the 1920s and '30s, when arctic fox or "white gold" was king. In a good winter, when the fox cycle was up, a trapper could become rich. A handful of these white trappers—Gus D'Aoust, George Magrum, Matt Murphy—still practised their trade in the 1950s. The very last of this generation of trappers were Fred Riddle and Ragnar Jonsson. Riddle was from Montana. He operated in the Dubawnt and upper Thelon river areas until 1976. The Swedish-born Jonsson trapped further east, around treeline at Nueltin Lake until 1980. Both men hung on in the Barren Lands into old age, Riddle till he was eighty and Jonsson to eighty-one. I've visited Riddle's main cabin, where he lived year-round. It's tiny, barely ten feet across, but Jonsson lived in a six-foot-diameter tipi, summer and winter alike.

In the mid-1970s a new generation of white men took up the isolated life of trapping in the Barrens. There were only three of them, and I met them all, quite by accident.

In July 1975 I came upon an abandoned tent camp, perched on an esker on the upper Hanbury River, that had obviously been occupied the preceding winter. Later, paddling into Fort Reliance at the east end of Great Slave Lake, I met and was befriended by a handsome young blond-haired man, Richard Black. The outfit I had come across on the Hanbury belonged to Richard and his partner, Lance Luebbert. Both Americans, they had spent the winter trapping on the Barrens and were looking for a better location for the following winter. I suggested the area where the Thelon flows into Lynx Lake from Whitefish Lake, specifically an esker on Lynx Lake. They eventually built a sixteen-by-sixteen-foot cabin there in 1978, which served as their base of operations for a number of years. During their summers they managed a fishing lodge at Fort Reliance.

Richard and Lance had great respect for that country. I remember visiting one of their outpost camps, where a few spruce trees grew in clumps. For firewood they had to cut some of these spruce, but instead of clear-cutting the closest clump, they selectively cut a tree or two here and there so there was no noticeable difference to each clump. I was impressed that they had been so careful.

I met the third young barrenland trapper in 1976. On August 30 of that year, Fred Brace and I finished a canoe trip on the upper Thelon south of Beaverhill Lake. By coincidence, the lake we were to fly out of was the same one Roger and Theresa Catling and their two-month-old daughter had just flown into the day before to spend the winter trapping. Their Twin Otter aircraft chartered out of Yellowknife couldn't access the exact place they wanted for their camp, so Fred and I ferried their entire outfit over to this location in our canoe.

On this spot stood the remains of a roomy log cabin built by Gus D'Aoust, one of the last of the old barrenland trappers. Roger had met Gus in Fort Reliance, where Roger's father, the meteorologist in Yellowknife, owned a summer cabin. Gus had retired to Fort Reliance after his stint in the Barrens and had fired Roger's imagination with tales of the Thelon country and the fur to be had there. It was also in Fort Reliance that Roger had met Theresa. She was the daughter of Noel Drybone, one of the last of the barrenland trappers and the head of the only Chipewyan family living in Reliance. Theresa had spent a number of winters on the Barrens trapping with her parents, including one when they nearly starved to death.

Roger, Theresa and their baby spent their first winter on the Thelon in an insulated tent, then built a comfortable plywood cabin on the same spot in 1977. That first winter, Roger had a team of Eskimo dogs supplied by Bill Carpenter of Yellowknife. The next winter, Roger substituted snowmobiles for the huskies so he could range further afield and run down wolves, his chief money-maker. The Catlings and their two daughters trapped on the Thelon for a number of years before Theresa tragically died of cancer in 1995 while still a young woman. Today, Roger continues to trap, but he has retreated to Fort Reliance, south of treeline.

Richard and Lance operated their trapline at Lynx Lake until 1993. Both now live more conventional lives back in the United States. Although I never saw Richard again after 1975, we kept in touch almost annually by letter. Richard's letters to me contain some telling, if laconic descriptions of a trapper's life. Here are a few excerpts:

January 16, 1979
...The fall weather could only be described as bleak. These conditions persisted until freeze-up on October 12...In general, the trapping on the Barrens was very lean this season. The fox run dried up after the caribou moved through in November and there was nothing left on the Barrens but arctic hare...

Lance and I returned [to Fort Reliance] January 12. There are good mink and marten around Reliance which will carry us through until we return for the spring hunt in March.

I'm only driving five dogs this season. Bill Carpenter has loaned me some huskies and they are strong. What normally requires six or seven dogs only takes five of Carpenter's huskies...

February 14, 1982
...It's been a hell of a cold winter. This year has not been too good for the fur business. The arctic fox population has been

right down. I haven't seen one yet. The caribou came by our place at Lynx Lake in late November. Sure was nice to see. There was an unusually high percentage of calves in the herd this year...

January 17, 1984
...Built a 16-by-20-foot log addition to the main cabin this fall. The cabin is now 16 by 36 feet—quite spacious. All fall we did not see any caribou. From September until November we were living on tuna casserole and lake trout. Freeze-up was late this year. The big lakes were not safe for travel until the second week of November. Things started happening here in mid-November. That's when the caribou started moving through our area from the east. There were many wolves and coloured foxes with them. Slim year for white fox. Last year we made our best hunt for white fox ever. With very little snow this winter, there are still many caribou on the Barrens...

January 10, 1985
...Extremely cold temperatures and lack of snow have limited our activities this winter...The caribou migrated through in the first week of November. The cold weather pushed them south of us into the trees quite rapidly...Roger dropped the mail off to us before Christmas and told us there are no caribou in Reliance so we will have to wait until the spring hunt...

February 18, 1986
...Roger Catling and family are on the Thelon and Lance and I at Lynx Lake. All of us are waiting for warmer weather. This morning it was −52°F here and at Roger's on the Thelon, which

is three hundred feet lower, it was −60°F. Even at noon the temperature stays below −40°F. Our cabin is plenty warm enough. We have plenty of grub and lots of good books so we are enjoying ourselves. Even our septic system and hand pump for the well below the cabin are still in operation...

Boy, have we got the snow this year. We have drifts around our cabin four or five feet high. Should be a good canoeing year for you...

December 26, 1992
...In general, you and I are never far apart. It's just that our paths never cross. My summers are still in Reliance at Trophy Lodge, but when September rolls around I get this migratory urge tugging me back to the Barrens and into the caribou again at Lynx Lake. I'm beginning to enjoy the winters more and more. The time is your own.

The Beverly herd has reached an incredible size. Part of the herd went through Lynx in late October. I've never seen so many lean caribou. They seemed stressed. Even the fall bulls were not fat. Lots of wolves, white fox and muskox. The Barrens seem full of game these days and it's great to see...

Richard's letters to me describe a way of life that has almost become a thing of the past. Canada may owe its very existence to the fur trade, but trapping is no longer a significant factor driving our economy, even in the North. Today, it's almost impossible to make a living as a trapper. For the most part, it's become a weekend activity practised by a few for extra income. Full-time trappers have become a rare breed indeed, and tend to belong to an older generation who are simply in love with their isolated and independent lifestyle in wild country.

John Hornby: Myth and Reality

One of the names most commonly associated with the Barren Lands, and especially the Thelon River, is John Hornby's. Hornby was an aristocratic English eccentric who starved to death on the Thelon in 1927, along with his eighteen-year-old cousin, Edgar Christian and another Englishman, Harold Adlard, who had joined them in Edmonton. The manner of Hornby's death ensured that his name would endure as a northern legend. The story is well known, and well told in young Edgar's published diary and in George Whalley's book, *The Legend of John Hornby*, where Hornby emerges as a controversial but heroic figure. To this day, the Hornby legend continues to inspire books and even music, plays and film documentaries.

Not everyone has been taken in by the Hornby saga, although credible critics are few and far between. One who surfaced more recently was the late Dr. Doug Clarke. He commented, in a paper written in 1978, "Much nonsense has been written about Hornby...He was hailed as an explorer, a rugged traveller and a northern expert after his death, but not before...He was not a well man or a strong man...and his capacity for living off the land did not approach that of the natives or white trappers. They liked him but pitied him. He made the cardinal error of not getting his meat when it was available. In spite of that, an Eskimo family could have lived where he starved."

Clarke, a biologist, spent two summers on the Thelon in the 1930s and while he was in the North he met most of Hornby's friends and acquaintances. He also knew all of the scientists and government officials of that time. Much of what I have written about Hornby here is based on Clarke's paper, a long, rambling account of his northern experiences, in which he apologized for having "to put old John Hornby in perspective." Clarke presented a shortened version of this paper at the Arctic Explorers Symposium in Toronto, but he mailed me the uncut version with some correspondence.

John Hornby was a remittance man who first came to the North in 1904. He was a wiry little fellow, part trapper, part trader, part explorer, but really none of these. He was an adventurer—a wanderer. As Clarke says, "He ended up as a victim of the explorer mystique." Hornby's friends in the North remembered him as restless, unpredictable and not very reliable—a man who always wanted to prove himself a tough guy. Although born into the English upper class, he affected no attitude of superiority. As barrenland trapper Allan Stewart once told Clarke, "Old John was a good guy. When he got his money [from England] everybody got drunk."

Hornby deliberately courted hardship. He would overwinter completely unprepared, with little more than some traps, a rifle, a fish net and a sack of flour. In the matter of survival, Hornby was always trying to "out-Indian the Indians," as he put it. He nearly starved to death a number of times while the Dene and white trappers lived in the same environment in relative comfort. Hornby certainly wasn't a planner or an organizer. He never learned, or so it seemed.

Through his trials and tribulations, Hornby proved time and again that he had the constitution to endure a rugged life in the northern wilderness. The question remains why he continued to gamble with his own life winter after winter when he must have known better. Was it all about his ego, which by some accounts was huge, or was he simply too much of an optimist?

The young John Hornby who arrived in Canada's North at the beginning of the last century was capable of impressive feats of travel and proved himself to be a reasonably successful trapper. However, according to his old friend George Douglas, Hornby was completely unskilled at hunting—a telling judgment in light of how he met his demise. Douglas also commented that, after Hornby was wounded in World War I, his physical condition deteriorated and he became more unpredictable than ever.

Upon his return to northern Canada following the war, Hornby encountered a small herd of muskoxen west of Artillery Lake on the edge of the Barrens. He learned from the Dene that numbers of muskoxen still survived on the Thelon River. By then, muskoxen had almost been wiped out on the Canadian mainland, and they were protected by law. Hornby knew the significance of the muskoxen on the Thelon, and he wanted to go there.

In 1924 Hornby and another eccentric Englishman, Captain James Critchell-Bullock, set off on a scientific and photographic expedition across the Barren Lands via the Thelon River. That winter they trapped foxes and wolves from a cave they had dug out of an esker north of treeline at Artillery Lake, then paddled down the Hanbury and Thelon rivers to Hudson Bay the next summer. It was a long, uncomfortable winter in their cave and according to each of them the other was quite mad. By the time they reached the Thelon, both were thin, weak and malnourished. However, they did manage to see and film some muskoxen.

Upon the recommendation of the government surveyor and northern explorer Guy Blanchet, O.S. Finnie, director of the Department of the Interior, had provided Hornby and Bullock with a small salary and financial help for their expedition in return for a report on the status of muskoxen and other wildlife along the Thelon. The following November, Hornby arrived in Ottawa after his trip down the Thelon, and Hoyes Lloyd, superintendent of wildlife protection at the Department of the Interior, sat him down to write a report on his expedition. Lloyd later told Doug Clarke that he practically had to kidnap Hornby and put him under lock and key in order to get that report. Lloyd was afraid that Hornby would wander off before he completed his obligations to the department, never to be seen again.

The way Clarke tells it, Finnie and Lloyd, along with Dr. R.M. Anderson of the National Museum, needed Hornby's report and recommendations for the game preserve they were already planning for the Thelon. A preserve recommended by someone who had never been there carried no weight. In the end, Hornby's brief report gave them just the leverage they needed. The Thelon Game Sanctuary was established on June 15, 1927, ironically just days after Edgar Christian, the last of the Hornby party, died of starvation on the Thelon River. Hornby has always been granted the lion's share of the credit for the creation of the sanctuary, but according to Doug Clarke's version of the events, Hornby actually did very little to deserve it.

In 1936 and '37 Clarke conducted a detailed biological investigation of the sanctuary. The Royal Canadian Mounted Police had buried the Hornby party beside their cabin on the Thelon in 1929 and had erected initialled wooden crosses at the head of each grave. At the request of Hornby's friend George Douglas, Clarke made a list of the animal dung on top of the three graves: muskox, caribou, wolf, arctic hare, ground squirrel, fox, lemming, ptarmigan and, just a few feet away, grizzly bear. Considering the wide variety of wildlife on the Thelon, many have since wondered how Hornby managed to starve to death. Appropriately, the working title of the book Hornby always claimed he would someday write was "In the Land of Feast or Famine."

In 1931 the story of the Hornby-Bullock expedition was told in *Snow Man*, a book by a young Californian, Malcolm Waldron.

Waldron had been intrigued by Bullock's tales of Hornby, and based his book on Bullock's diaries. In my opinion, however, neither Waldron nor Whalley, in his *Legend of John Hornby*, ever fully understood Hornby's behaviour, because neither author had ever travelled in the Barren Lands. For someone like me, Hornby's motivations are not entirely mysterious. He was in love with the country, pure and simple, and he just couldn't stay away.

The place where Hornby lived and died on the Thelon now bears the official name of Hornby Point. On my early visits to Hornby Point I used to wonder if I was being confronted by Hornby's ghost because of some of the unusual things that happened to us there. Once, a lone caribou—and the only one we encountered on our trip—passed within ten feet of us at the graves. On another occasion, a grumpy bull muskox chased me around a large spruce tree beside the cabin, and one night a white wolf paced back and forth on the shore in front of the cabin and howled for hours.

Because I visit Hornby Point more frequently than anyone else— I've been there more than fifty times now—I think of myself as the unofficial keeper of the graves. One spring in the 1980s, a load of wet snow slid off a spruce tree behind Harold Adlard's grave and broke the cross. I tied it back up with fishing line, but by the mid-1990s only Edgar Christian's cross remained intact. In 1996 I took the exact measurements of each cross and told my clients that someday, when it became appropriate, I intended to replace them. The next winter two of my American clients, Barry and Fred Goldstein, mailed me US$100 for the replacements. That forced my hand. Joe Bird of Fort Smith fashioned replicas of the originals from red cedar, and in July 1997 I laid them flat on stones on top of each grave. When the old crosses finally disintegrate, I'll set up the new ones.

PART V

Family Connections

Impressing Lia

It seems I've always had a way with wolves. I've had a lot of luck running into them, I'm skilful at finding their dens, and I've always been able to communicate with them easily. Because I know wolves are completely harmless, whenever I meet them face to face I'm always relaxed and completely trustful. If wolves can read my body language, I'll never have anything but wonderful experiences with them.

A lot of the appeal of interacting with wolves is talking to them and having them talk back. Wolves love to howl, and they'll often respond to anything that sounds even remotely like a wolf. In my wolf research days in Algonquin Park we had wolves howl back at such unlikely sounds as music playing on radios or the slam of a car door on a quiet night. There was one pack that had a rendezvous site about a mile from a boys' camp on Source Lake. I remember sitting in my canoe on more than one quiet evening when the bugler at the camp played taps—followed shortly thereafter by the entire pack of wolves responding in full song. Although you don't have to sound very much like a wolf to make them howl, it certainly helps if you do.

Sometimes when I've howled at wolves they've come right to me. This happened twice on a canoe trip in late August of 1981. As it turned out, my timing was impeccable, because that was the trip when I met my wife, Lia. I wasn't showing off, but the wolves seemed to be going out of their way to make me look good.

Our first contact came just at sundown one clear, quiet evening when I thought I heard a wolf howl way off in the distance. When I howled back, we heard four or five wolves and a number of pups respond faintly about two miles down the shore of the lake we were camped on. About every twenty minutes we'd exchange howls again, and each time they'd be a little closer. We kept this conversation going until after dark. In the end, the wolves were howling in full chorus within two hundred yards of us and in the morning we found their tracks in the sand right inside our camp kitchen. It was pretty impressive stuff. Lia thought so, anyway.

Several days later, we crossed treeline and continued through the open white spruce forests of the northern taiga. We had just gathered for breakfast one morning when a number of wolves and their pups broke out in a spontaneous howl only three or four hundred yards behind our camp. When I howled back there was no reply, but within seconds we saw half a dozen adults and pups running through the trees towards us. As soon as they saw us, they beat a hasty retreat.

Lia was even more impressed with that performance because it happened in broad daylight and it proved the first one wasn't a fluke. There was a lot more substance in the development of our relationship, of course, but first impressions are important. It seems that wolves have influenced the course of my life in a number of ways. I think I could add Lia and, by extension, my sons Graham and Evan to that list, as well.

Graham's Beach

In August 1989 Lia was returning from one of our canoe trips in the Barren Lands in a Cessna 185 float plane piloted by Terry Trytten. Just as they approached treeline the aileron on the right wing of the airplane came loose and almost fell off. Terry immediately made preparations for an emergency landing and, as part of this procedure, he was able to radio their location and the nature of their problem to a high-flying intercontinental jet on a polar route. The jet, in turn, relayed this information to Fort Smith, and another Cessna was dispatched to go to their aid. Terry made a safe landing and in an interesting coincidence happened to come down on a river that we had canoed many times. In fact, they ended up marooned on a beach only a mile from where I had howled the wolf pack into our camp in August 1981. The location also happens to be one of the most stunningly beautiful places in the North.

Only after she returned to Fort Smith did Lia find out how serious their situation had been. Without a functioning aileron, Terry could have lost control of the aircraft, and they might have died that day in that beautiful place.

That close call prompted my wife to appraise her life and reach a major decision. We had been married five years, and she was almost thirty-nine. If she was ever going to have children, she decided, she'd better get on with it. As a result, Graham was born less than a year later, and Evan less than two years after Graham.

In 1993 my guiding season ended earlier than usual. With a bit of summer still left in late August, Lia and I decided to take the boys on a canoe trip to one of our favourite places—the river where Lia had made her emergency landing. At the time, Graham was three and Evan was sixteen months, so the trip was more camping and relaxing on the beaches than it was canoeing. About the only time of the day we ever got to travel by canoe was for a few hours in the early afternoon, when the boys liked to nap.

One lovely afternoon late in the trip, we found ourselves paddling towards the beach where Lia had been marooned on the stricken aircraft four years earlier. Graham was sound asleep in the middle of the canoe, lying on a pack as we returned to the place where the idea of Graham had begun. This was an important place in our little family's history, a place of life and near-death.

As we approached the beach, Graham suddenly rolled over the gunwale of the canoe into the river. He wore a life preserver, and I easily fished him out of the water as he floated by the stern. Understandably, he was very upset from this rude awakening. At the time, I thought it was pretty spooky that Graham had rolled into the river at that particular time and place, especially since it was the only time on the trip that he fell out of the canoe. I still think of it as a baptism of sorts.

More Bear Stories

I don't know what was wrong with the bears around Fort Smith in 1993. Perhaps there was a failure in the berry crop. Whatever the reason, they were all over town all summer long. Dozens were live-trapped or shot on the streets. It seemed that nearly everyone had a bear story. Here are three of the best.

In early September, Karl Hoffman flew his Super Cub float plane out to one of the cabins on his trapline to do some carpentry work. The cabin is on a lake about eighty miles northeast of Fort Smith. In the wee hours of the next morning, Karl was awakened by the yapping of his little house dog and something thumping on one of the cabin windows. A large black bear was trying to force its way inside. Karl didn't have a gun with him, but he managed to scare the bear off and he turned the radio up loud in hopes the noise would keep the bear away. However, the bear kept coming back and trying to get in through the window.

Karl remembered that he had an axe leaning against the cabin just outside the door. But when he opened the door a crack to try to reach the axe, his little dog slipped outside. In no time, the bear made off with the dog into the bush surrounding the cabin. Karl was so upset by this turn of events that he rushed out of the cabin in an effort to save his pet. Not only was there an axe leaning against the cabin, there was also a needle bar. (A needle bar is a heavy six-foot-long iron bar with a pointed end, used for opening up a hole in the lake ice in winter.)

Karl is a big, strong man. He grabbed the needle bar and took off into the bush where he'd seen the bear disappear with his dog in its jaws. No sooner had Karl entered the bush than the bear charged him. This was no bluff charge. The bear came right at Karl! Karl stopped the bear cold when he shoved the needle bar deep into the animal's chest. The bear backed up, then charged again. Karl rammed the bar deep into the bear a second time. This time the bear retreated into the bush and disappeared.

The little dog was dead, and with an aggressive wounded bear on the loose, Karl ran to his airplane and flew over to his main trapping cabin, where he kept a rifle. When he returned to the other cabin, he couldn't find the bear, so he slept there again that night. Early the next morning, the bear was there again, trying to get into the cabin through the same window. That was the bear's last mistake. Karl shot it.

Dave Powder's trapline lies south of Karl's. That same fall, Dave was at one of his trapping cabins chopping wood when a black bear grabbed him from behind. The bear had Dave's foot in its mouth and was dragging him off when Peaches, Dave's big malamute, broke her chain and charged the bear. The bear dropped Dave's foot and turned its attention on the attacking husky. That gave Dave the opportunity to run to his cabin, where he retrieved his rifle and shot the bear. Dave credits Peaches with saving his life.

In late September of that year, my family and I, along with my good friend Kevin Antoniak, were on our annual moose hunt in the same general area as the traplines owned by Karl and Dave. Lia and I had both our toddlers with us—this was a month after the events at "Graham's Beach." We set up a big canvas wall tent, and Kevin had a small sleeping tent for himself. Moose hunting isn't much different from canoe tripping, except you're in a canoe from dawn to dusk—calling and looking for moose—and you return to a base camp every night.

The second day of the hunt was a beautiful warm autumn day with the leaves in full colour. After lunch at camp, Kevin and I took Graham hunting with us for an hour or two in the canoe. Lia decided that she and little Evan would have a nap in the wall tent while we were gone. Lia had just dozed off when she was awakened by a tearing sound. Three feet above her head was the face of a black bear looking down at her through a hole in the roof.

Lia yelled, then scrambled over to the door of the tent. The bear was standing just outside. Lia has never wanted anything to do with guns, but Kevin had left her a "bear-scarer," which is simply a big firecracker. Lia lit the bear-scarer and threw it out the door. When it exploded, the bear ran off. However, it soon returned. After she got the bear to back off a second time by banging two pots together, Lia snatched up Evan and ran down onto the big wide-open sand beach in front of the tent. Every time the bear started down the beach towards her, Lia would bang the pots together and the bear would retreat to the vicinity of the tent. Since Kevin and I had the only canoe, she and Evan were stranded on the beach with an aggressive bear that challenged them repeatedly.

Kevin and I returned with Graham about an hour after Lia had run down to the beach. As soon as I saw Lia there holding the two pots, I knew she had a bear problem. She quickly told us about the bear's aggressive nature and said she'd last seen it at the wall tent. When Kevin and I approached the tent with our rifles, the bear was nowhere to be seen. Slowly and carefully, Kevin went one way around the tent while I went around the other. Kevin had just reached the back corner of the tent when he saw the bear facing him about fifteen feet away. He had raised his rifle to fire a shot over the bear's head when suddenly the animal was coming at him. He killed it with one shot when it was only a few feet away.

The bear was rather small and thin. We thought it was a young one until we examined its teeth, which were worn and decayed. This was an old bear that was malnourished, perhaps starving. It had obviously been testing Lia and Evan as potential prey. We were lucky that bear hadn't come along when Kevin and I were away from camp for several hours, as we often were. I've run into hundreds of black bears over the years, but that's the only aggressive one I've ever encountered. It's also the only bear we've ever been forced to kill, and I hope it's the last.

PART VI

Some Favourite Places

The Most Beautiful River

The most beautiful river in the Barren Lands isn't my favourite. I didn't discover it until the mid-1980s and, like a lot of loves in your life, I suppose, you have a softer spot for the earlier ones. But there's no denying this river's staggering beauty. It's in a class by itself. No other river comes even close.

The most beautiful river in the Barren Lands is my secret. For eight years only my clients and I canoed it. Then one of my clients revealed its location and others go there now.

My secret river is clear as glass and full of rapids. It boils through canyons and braids through gravel bars. Rugged hills, sand dunes and eskers rise steeply above it. Numerous streams gush in from narrow canyons cut through the stony hills, and sheltered in its valley are clumps of spruce trees and thickets of willow.

Dozens of peregrines nest along my secret river. There are white gyrfalcons, large numbers of Canada geese, many species of ducks—indeed, birds of all kinds. The river valley is a favourite of denning wolves and home to as many grizzlies as anywhere else in the

Barrens. Large numbers of caribou pass through at least twice a year. There are muskoxen and even moose. In contrast to the virtual moonscape of the surrounding black-lichen tundra, the valley of my secret river is a lush paradise, teeming with wildlife.

I know that a small number of people reading even these few words will recognize this river. I hope they can understand the value of protecting its location. The most beautiful river in the Barren Lands is more beautiful when you have it all to yourself.

Thelon River

The Thelon is a big, sandy, clear-water river with a strong current but few rapids. For 750 miles, it cuts its way across the pristine heartland of one of the last great wildernesses left on earth. The Thelon has many outstanding features, but by far its most unusual is the luxuriant oasis of trees and tall shrubs growing along the middle section of the river, far north of the regular treeline. This oasis, in turn, gives birth to the greatest variety and abundance of birds and mammals in the Barren Lands. The Thelon valley is legendary as a wildlife paradise—as a land of beauty and wonder—long known to the Chipewyan Dene as God's country, as the birthplace of animals and, when the world was created, as the place where God began.

The Thelon is a river of superlatives. Rising at treeline and terminating at tidewater in Hudson Bay, it has the largest drainage basin and the greatest flow of any river on the tundra. Because of its distance from the Arctic and Hudson Bay coasts, the upper half of the river, in the south-central Barrens, enjoys the best summer weather north of treeline. Of all the major tundra rivers, the Thelon is the most isolated but the easiest to canoe. Its scenic variety is unparalleled. No other arctic river has such a long and legendary human history. Nowhere else is the wildlife as rich. In recognition of its exceptional characteristics, the Government of Canada designated almost four hundred miles of the remote Thelon as a Heritage River in 1990.

Although the Thelon lies on the Canadian Shield, most of the river flows through a sandstone belt, a younger formation deposited on top of the old bedrock foundation. Because sandstone is soft and easily eroded by water, the Thelon is evenly graded, with relatively few rapids or lakes. Originating in a cluster of big tundra lakes close to treeline, the Thelon runs almost completely uninterrupted for over three hundred miles before entering another series of large lakes on its lower reaches. Two of these lower lakes—Aberdeen and Baker—are more than fifty miles in length.

The upper parts of the watershed are coursed by big, treed, sandy eskers, the largest and most spectacular on the continent. Up to 250 miles long and hundreds of feet in height, these eskers dominate the landscape and add incredible richness and scenic variety to the entire region. Eskers are the inverted beds of long-dead rivers that flowed under the melting glaciers some nine thousand years ago. Usually, they form a single ridge of sand and gravel, but sometimes they fan out into multiple ridges or extensive areas of sand dunes. The surfaces of these long, sinuous ridges are mosaics of eroded runs of stark white sand and patchwork mats of surprisingly lush green vegetation. Scattered along their sandy heights are spike-shaped spruce trees and below their sheltered flanks more substantial stands of robust spruce and tamarack. Everywhere, there are aquamarine ponds and small lakes with beaches all around. The eskers of the upper Thelon combine such a striking array of features that they almost seem to belong to a surreal, fairy-tale world.

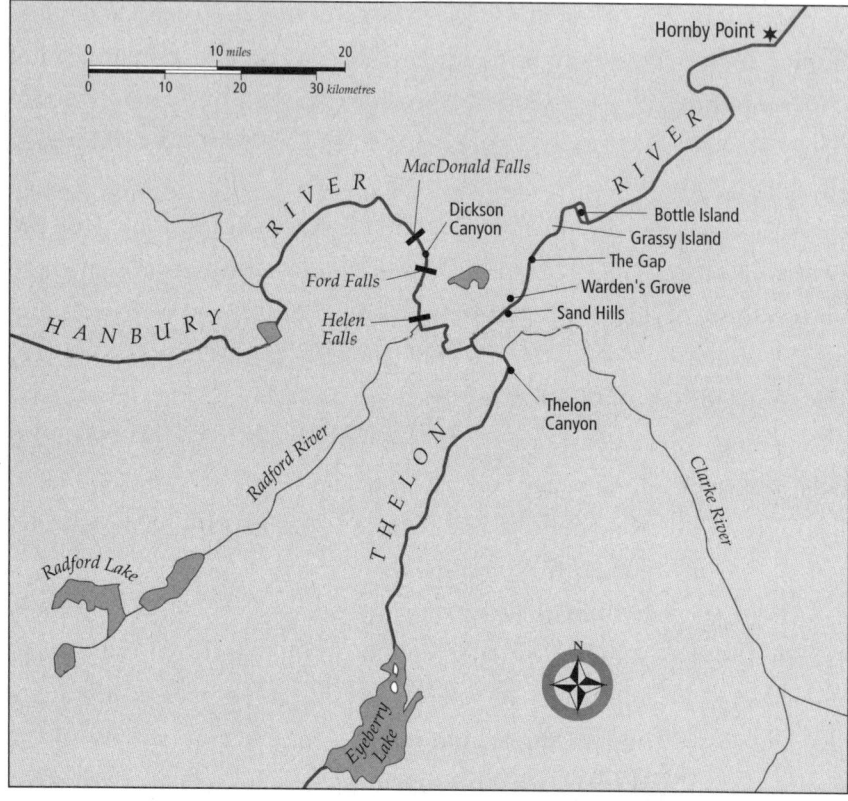

The central part of the Thelon basin contains what is reputed to be the largest drumlin field in the world. Created during the last glaciation, the Thelon drumlins line up in a series of parallel, cigar-shaped ridges that run for miles. These drumlins are so straight that when viewed from a low-flying float plane, they appear man-made.

Along the middle portion of the Thelon, almost dead centre in the Barren Lands, the Thelon Oasis follows the course of the river for 160 miles from the Clarke River junction to Ursus Islands. Here, in the vastness of the treeless tundra, a thin ribbon of scattered spruce stands and extensive thickets of willow, dwarf birch

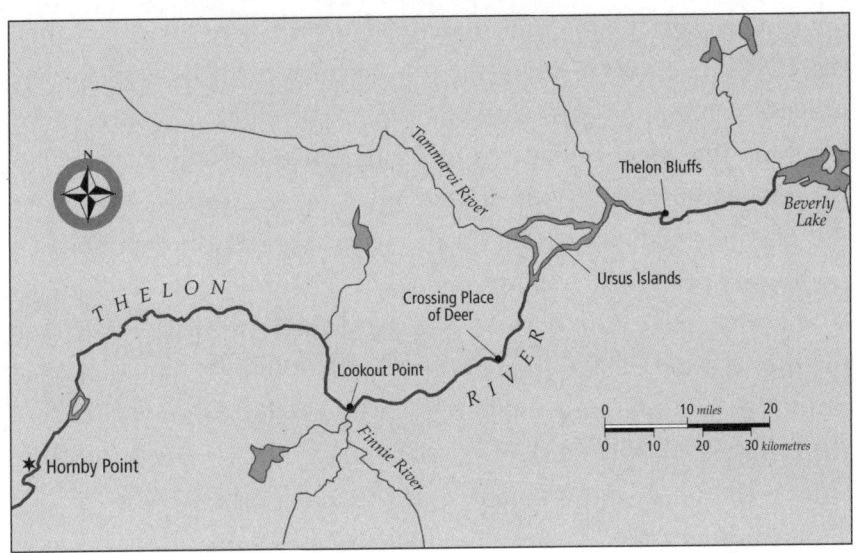

and alder line both banks of the river. There are even a few trembling aspen and balsam poplar in places, as well as raspberries, currants and columbine, hundreds of miles north of where you'd expect to find them.

In contrast to the boreal forest, the Thelon Oasis shows no evidence of fire. The spruce that grow are as old as spruce can be. Along little creeks spilling into the Thelon there are white spruce up to a thousand years old, reaching more than three feet in diameter. During a period of warmer climate over four thousand years ago, the oasis was part of the northern treeline. These isolated trees are still found here today because summers are significantly warmer along this stretch of the river valley than on the surrounding tundra. Summers are warmer because of the low elevation of the oasis, its deep interior location and the absence of big, cold lakes.

The middle Thelon River and its oasis bisect the Thelon Wildlife Sanctuary, created in 1927 to conserve "wildlife in general and muskox in particular." Known as the Thelon Game Sanctuary until the 1990s, it remains one of the very few places in the North where mineral exploration and development are prohibited. Representing less than 5 percent of the Barren Lands, this sanctuary nevertheless contains more than 21,000 square miles, or an area equal in size to the province of Nova Scotia. It also carries the distinction of being the largest protected area in Canada.

In providing a safe haven for some of the last muskox herds left on the mainland of Canada, the Thelon Wildlife Sanctuary has proved to be a monumental success. The recolonization of much of the Barren Lands by muskoxen in recent decades is directly attributable to the herds that originated in this sanctuary. With its unique spruce outliers, the Thelon River valley is also home to such forest-dwelling mammals as beaver, otter, porcupine, red squirrel and moose, all of which are found here some two hundred miles north of the normal limit of their range. In fact, the oasis supports the largest population of moose north of the continuous forest. Similarly, dozens of species of birds normally associated with the boreal forest are found along the Thelon in the heart of the tundra. To date, we have recorded 103 bird species in the sanctuary and have confirmed sixty-four species as breeding there. Raptors such as bald and golden eagles, gyrfalcons and peregrines are probably more abundant here than anywhere else in the Barrens. The Thelon is also North America's most important moulting ground for the larger subspecies of Canada geese.

The Thelon Wildlife Sanctuary includes important parts of the range and calving grounds of the 275,000-strong Beverly caribou herd. Indeed, four caribou herds (the Beverly, Qamanirjuaq, Bathurst and Ahiak herds), with a combined population of well over one million animals, use portions of the Thelon watershed in their annual migrations. Along with such large ungulate populations come some of the world's healthiest populations of top predators—tundra wolves, wolverines and barren-ground grizzlies. Former Canadian Wildlife Service biologist, John Kelsall, who was in charge of the extensive studies on barren-ground caribou in the 1950s, believed the Thelon valley contained the largest numbers of denning wolves in the North.

With its unique blend of boreal and tundra birds and mammals, the Thelon River goes unchallenged as the premier wildlife area on the Canadian tundra. On our canoe trips there we have encountered all of the five large mammal species—caribou, muskoxen, wolves, moose and grizzlies—during the course of a single day. Some days we have been blessed with a dozen wolves, a hundred muskoxen or a hundred thousand caribou.

Before it was explored, little more than a hundred years ago, the Thelon River was the last major blank spot on the map of the mainland of North America. Large parts of this watershed remained terra incognita until airplanes arrived in the 1930s. Most of it remained unmapped until the 1960s. Today, the upper and middle parts of the Thelon River are more distant from human settlements and roads than any other location on our continent.

Despite its remoteness, the Thelon has a surprisingly rich and well-documented archaeological and historical record, dating back some eight thousand years. In his book *Thelon: A River Sanctuary*, my friend David Pelly summed up what we know of that human history with these words: "No other northern river has a history like the Thelon's. No other river has drawn such a range of travellers to it. No other river has produced such legends. Only the Thelon."

I have paddled dozens of rivers across the Barren Lands—most of the famous ones and some known only to me or a select few—but none have the allure and mystique of the Thelon. The Thelon draws me back again and again. To my mind, the Thelon is the quintessence of wilderness—the jewel in the crown—and home to the most beautiful places left on earth. For me, the Thelon is a spiritual place, an inviolable sanctum, secreted away in the heart of the wild.

The Place of Power

If there are more beautiful places on this earth than the big, treed eskers of the upper Thelon River watershed, I have yet to see them. As you travel north, the eskers thin out, but just southwest of the geographical centre of the Barren Lands, on the western edge of the Thelon Oasis, the landscape is particularly striking. Beginning at the Thelon Canyon and a high esker to the northeast, this heartland extends down the Thelon past the confluence of the Clarke and Hanbury rivers, past the Sand Hills, Warden's Grove and the Gap to Grassy Island, Bottle Island and the big hills beyond; it encompasses the lower Hanbury River, with its eskers and sand dunes, from MacDonald Falls and Dickson Canyon down to Helen Falls and the junction of the Radford River.

This is a place where elements come together—where rivers meet, where the hard rock of the Precambrian Shield joins the sandstone of the Thelon valley and where extensive stands of spruce trees and forest-based birds and mammals mingle with the plants and animals of the tundra. Here stony hills give way to the lush complexity of the Thelon Oasis.

Before the white man, this was a meeting place of men and herds in summer. Aboriginal peoples were drawn to the caribou crossings along this part of the Thelon for thousands of years. Great herds of caribou still pass through this area in unbelievable numbers on their way south in July.

Today, this section of the Thelon River is about as remote as it's possible to get on this continent. The few who are privileged to travel to this secluded spot seldom fail to be profoundly moved by its majesty. There's something about the isolation and purity of this place, the sweep and scale of the country and the variety of life and landforms. There's something about the ancient human connections and the way things come together, beginning and ending in this place. There's a spiritual presence here. You can feel the power.

The Oasis by Canoe

Some excerpts from my camp diary

July 25

We are camped at the head of the three-mile Thelon Canyon, above the Clarke River junction, at a place considered by some to be the most spectacular scene on the Thelon River. By convention, the Thelon Oasis begins just below this sandstone canyon and runs downriver to Ursus Islands, but a case could be made that it extends much further upstream. Tomorrow we enter the oasis, but first we must make a two-mile portage here along the eastern rim of the canyon. We have agreed on a 5 a.m. wake-up call so we can finish the portage before the afternoon heat.

Earlier this evening, around eight o'clock, blackflies emerged in large numbers when the wind died. My clients have all gone to bed early. The evening sun is low in the northwest as I walk downriver to an overlook where most of the canyon comes into view. The eastern wall and part of the river are bathed in a brilliant, golden light, and here what was only a deep rumble at camp is a powerful roar. Below me is a maelstrom of rapids, chutes and low curtain falls.

Despite the blackflies, the magnificence of this place—with the water and light flying below—casts its spell. I reflect on the previous seven days of our journey and I have every reason to be pleased. One evening, a white wolf walked by all ten of us—only twenty paces away—while we were eating our supper. It scarcely gave us a glance. The next evening, another wolf came to inspect our tents and passed within twenty-five feet of one of my clients. In addition to these, there have been many more encounters with wildlife, including another nine wolves at two active dens, five moose and well over one hundred muskoxen.

While I am still lost in my thoughts, the sun sinks behind the distant hills. The spell is broken as the canyon below me is enveloped in shadows and loses its lustre. I turn back towards camp under the fiery glow of a cloudless sky that promises another beautiful day.

July 26 & 27
We divide the portage into four parts and shuttle everything over in three or four loads apiece. The wind is light and the blackflies numerous, so we keep our headnets on. Once back on the river, we paddle, wade and line our five canoes down the remainder of the canyon to where the first big stands of white spruce trees grow. Along the way, we encounter four active peregrine falcon aeries.

A few miles below the canyon, we come to the last obstruction on the river—intimidating rows of big rolling waves and vertical sandstone cliffs on each side. We sneak through along the left shore, then follow the wall of sandstone to the outflow of the Hanbury River, where the Thelon turns north again. Here, the Thelon widens to over half a mile and the land opens up. We can now see great distances. The far-off high hills on the horizons are sharp in the blazing sun. Through a land of greens and tans, the big blue river glides on under a gigantic dome of azure sky. The only sound is the wind.

The vegetation is changing. The river valley is lush—a land of plenty, of tall grass and big thickets of willow. The tundra still reaches the river in places, but now there are stands of large spruce trees above the riverbanks.

The land is also rich in birds. Colonies of arctic terns claim the gravel bars and low sandy islands as their own and defend them against all comers. There are gulls, sandpipers, plovers, ducks, tundra swans, red-throated loons and bald eagles. Most of the Canada geese have now finished their moult and are migrating downriver in large flocks.

We paddle by the Sand Hills on the east shore, where numerous fresh caribou trails are visible. The big sand beach on the west side of the river has been beaten down by the hooves of thousands of animals that swam the Thelon here on their southward migration a few days ago. Downstream, windrows of white winter hair, which the caribou have shed as they crossed the river, stretch for miles along the shoreline.

A few stragglers from the herd are still loitering along the river, mostly lost calves and animals with a noticeable limp. These are destined to be caught and consumed by wolves or grizzlies in a matter of days. There are also a few cow caribou pacing the riverbanks in search of their calves that have drowned or gone astray during the confusion of the river crossing. We watch one cow sniff a lost calf, then bunt it away with her head when she realizes it's not hers. These separated cows and calves come readily to my imitations of their calls for close-up photography.

Where the river funnels through the bare hills of the Gap it slows and deepens. I focus my binoculars on a pile of sticks on the scree of the steepest slope, where golden eagles often nest. The nest is empty this year. Once we pass through the Gap, the land opens up again. There are big, stony hills up ahead that appear grey. On our left, a great sweep of white sand runs downriver and out of sight; a little farther on it will merge with the ten-foot-high willow jungles of Grassy Island. On our right the green slopes of big tundra hills loom up from the river above more sand beaches. The scale of the country is huge.

As the main channel of the river swings around Grassy Island it widens and shallows. The bottom is pure white sand. The sun on the clear water creates bands of blues and greens reflecting the varying depths of the sandbars in the river. Images of the Caribbean flit through my mind.

Across the river from Grassy Island we pass extensive forests of thick spruce. We see three more moose and a solitary bull muskox. At Bottle Island we suddenly come upon a densely packed herd of some two thousand caribou on the mainland. They are standing shoulder to shoulder on the beach and on the low sand dunes behind. We photograph them, going as close as we want without disturbing them, then make camp a mile farther downstream. Later that evening these same animals cross to Bottle Island, then swim the river again into our campsite. From a prominent knoll, we watch them form a long, thin line as they file up and away through the big tundra hills. Finally, they are swallowed up by the immensity of the landscape.

July 28 & 29
Over the next two days we travel to Hornby Point through the most heavily forested part of the river. Although the tundra is seldom in sight, it's never more than a short walk away. The weather stays clear and hot with good breezes to keep the blackflies at bay. The summer was late getting started, but now the Thelon is warm and the swimming is delicious.

We see many boreal birds, including a pair of merlins that have nested in the same spruce tree for years. We make our usual stop at a place I call "Garnet Falls," on a small creek near the Thelon. In this little spot, there are plants that are normally associated with more southern locations. Some white spruce trees grow so large in this part of the oasis that a man cannot reach around their trunks. There are also some stunted balsam poplar and one stand of trembling aspen with trees up to ten inches in diameter. The nearest aspens I've seen to these ones are considerably south of treeline, about 250 miles away.

On a walk in the hills, one of my clients finds a perfect quartzite spear point near some old tent rings. The edges are serrated, and seem as sharp as they must have been the day they were crafted. Unlike most of our finds, this spear point is side-notched, which means it's probably no more than a thousand years old. We find it lying fully exposed on the surface, as if its owner had just dropped it there the day before. Such discoveries are infrequent. Broken points, on the other hand, are common finds in the heaps of quartzite chips covering many of the hilltops along this part of the Thelon.

Wildlife continues to be abundant. We see more scattered caribou, eight muskoxen and six moose. At one traditional wolf den, a big white male and a tawny-coloured female emerge from an entrance after I howl. I recognize them from previous years. They trot up on top of a little ridge less than one hundred yards away and howl at us for a while. There are signs of pups at the den, but they stay out of sight. The next morning we find that the wolves have pulled a fast one. It's their old trick: overnight, they moved the pups to a second den a mile downriver. I anticipated this and we find them there with two pups.

July 30
As usual, we are at up at seven, breakfast at eight and on the water by nine. First, we make the obligatory stop at the Hornby cabin and graves. The caved-in cabin stands only three or four logs high. Over the years, canoeists have taken every souvenir possible from the derelict cabin. Since I was here last, someone has removed the door hinges.

Past Hornby Point, the Thelon narrows and speeds up considerably. Wide gravel and stone beaches—light tan, light grey or golden—line much of the river from here all the way down to Beverly Lake. The forest thins out to become scattered trees. Although some consider the eastern terminus of the oasis to lie just a few miles below Hornby Point, there is no biological basis for this argument. Boreal birds and mammals are found all the way down to Ursus Islands, just west of Beverly Lake. From a low-flying aircraft it is also evident that the Thelon valley beyond Hornby Point is much more heavily forested than is apparent to a canoeist from the river.

In the afternoon we find two young gyrfalcons in a stick nest at the top of a spruce tree. Even though they are almost full grown, these birds are still covered in white fluff. Most gyrfalcons are fledged by mid-July, so this is an extremely late brood.

By the time we make camp at 4 p.m., we have covered twenty-seven miles and have seen nine muskoxen. It's another sunny day with the temperature still over 80°F as we put up our tents. Afterwards, we take a long, languid swim.

July 31
We are blessed again with clear, breezy weather, and the Thelon is even faster than the day before. Sandstone cliffs, fifty feet in height, are prominent along this part of the river. Every cliff has its resident pair of rough-legged hawks, which give a piercing cry as they soar high above us. One cliff also turns up a pair of peregrine falcons. We see seven more muskoxen, a few caribou and a red fox. Although the carpets of early summer flowers are long gone, the rock beaches are often pink with low arctic fireweed, a favoured forage of muskoxen. Everywhere beyond the beaches, berries lie underfoot. There are crowberries, bearberries, cranberries, cloudberries and blueberries. Only some cloudberries have ripened, but the geese are already feeding on them in large numbers.

In mid-afternoon I catch a glimpse of what appears to be a wolf den that I haven't noticed in previous years. It's above a high bank, and we climb up for a look. On top, two adult wolves and a big black pup walk up to within twenty feet of us as we crouch in some willows. They disappear into the bushes without a sound when they finally discover us, and we get a good look at two more adults and another pup a little further on at the den.

August 1
Today, the land flattens out to Lookout Point, where the topography changes again. There are two pingos along this piece of the Thelon and we view one of them from a distance. In this flat terrain the sky is enormous. From little knolls only twenty feet above the river, it seems like we can see forever. From one vantage point we notice some far-off buttes. They seem out of place in the Barren Lands. The Thelon braids into several channels, and tall willow thickets go on for miles. Back behind the river there are a few patches of spruce forest. This is good moose country, but today we see none. Our muskox count is five.

Almost a mile away, on a straight stretch of the river, I spot a grizzly feeding on a bull muskox lying in the shallows near shore. The wind is unfavourable, blowing our scent towards the bear. We try to approach by paddling along the opposite shore of the river channel, but the grizzly winds us at five hundred yards and runs off.

August 2
Beyond Lookout Point the landscape is more hilly and the stands of spruce are larger and more frequent. This is one of my favourite stretches of the Thelon. The weather is still clear, but there's some smoke in the air from distant forest fires. At a blowout I show the others some scattered spear points and knives that are thousands of years old. We pass nine scattered bull muskoxen and spend an hour, unnoticed, with a herd of forty-seven that contains only one calf. As usual, they are all on the north side of the river. A little further on, one of my most reliable wolf dens proves to be unoccupied.

We camp at the base of John Kelsall's lookout hill near the

Crossing Place of Deer. On top of the lookout, great vistas of tundra open up before us across the river. Downstream, we can see the last substantial patch of forest of the oasis and the big, blue hills beyond Ursus Islands, some twenty miles away.

August 3
The barometer is falling. The first dark clouds of the trip move in on us with a few small showers. The day is warm and the wind is light. The blackflies are bothersome even on the water. We pass through Ursus Islands, a low area where the Thelon divides around a huge island of willow. It's a great place for moose, and we come upon five of them.

In Ursus Islands we briefly look for a wolf den, the presence of which I have suspected for years. Each summer I widen my search. This time we are lucky. A heavily tracked area soon leads us to the den, where we surprise a sleeping white wolf. One pup peeks out at us from an entrance after I howl.

Just downstream, we overtake a platinum-blond grizzly walking down a sand beach. It appears to be a young bear, recently separated from its mother. For the next forty-five minutes this bear remains on the beach watching us. We paddle very close, confident of our safety in the deep water. The grizzly stands up frequently on its hind legs, but shows neither aggression nor fear. We take hundreds of photographs before we move on.

Later in the afternoon, a northeast wind rises and blows the blackflies away. During a short break, I lie back on my canoe with my feet up on the gunwales and steer with my paddle. I feel my paddle bumping and, thinking it must be striking the river bottom, I look over the side to see only deep water. As I sit up, a giant lake trout rises out of the depths and repeatedly strikes my paddle. It does this about twenty times before I finally smack it and chase it away. This happened to me once before many years ago, and it makes me think twice about going for a swim.

We camp in a majestic place in the big, green hills below Ursus Islands where we can watch another herd of muskoxen feeding and sleeping across the river. We are now beyond the oasis on the wide-open tundra. Nearby are the remains of many Inuit camps that date back as far as the late nineteenth century. Downriver, it's only a short day's travel through the hills to Beverly Lake. Our chartered float planes are to meet us there in three days.

PART VII

Changes

Wildlife and Land Use

There have been many important changes in the Barren Lands and northern forests since I spent my first summer there in 1971. The quality of wilderness has deteriorated in some regions, forest fires have ravaged large areas and the distribution and abundance of birds and mammals on the tundra, in particular, have gone through some radical changes. Some of the changes in wildlife populations have roots that go back over a century or more; some may be the result of natural cycles. Others, however, may have been induced by more recent trends, such as global warming.

Generally speaking, the large mammals of the Barren Lands have fared well in recent decades. Muskoxen, moose and grizzlies have expanded their ranges, and populations of all large mammals (including wolverines) have grown, with the exception of muskoxen and perhaps tundra wolves in some sectors. This general increase in large mammal numbers on the mainland tundra follows closely on the heels of the last major exodus of aboriginal peoples off the land in the 1950s and coincides with the decreasing importance of trapping in the northern economy. These changes in lifestyle have undoubtedly been beneficial for wildlife over immense areas of real estate in the North.

By the 1970s the huge interior of the Barren Lands was almost completely uninhabited by man. Over the previous two centuries, smallpox and other diseases, the fur trade, the dwindling of the great caribou herds and the more recent establishment of northern communities had either taken a direct toll on aboriginal populations or had acted as an irresistible force, luring them away from the old caribou-dependent way of life in the Barren Lands. With current human populations largely confined to a number of communities well south of treeline and along the Arctic and Hudson Bay coasts, there have probably been few other periods since the end of the last glaciation when the mainland tundra was so empty of people.

It was into this vast uninhabited wilderness that I disappeared for several months each summer in the early 1970s, paddling and portaging through a network of river systems to the Arctic Ocean or Hudson Bay. A handful of others were doing the same. For a few summers at least, we felt like lions in our own private paradise, masters of all we surveyed. Land use in the Barren Lands was in a vacuum in those days. The very last of the Inuit, Dene and barrenland trappers still living independently out on the land were vanishing, mineral exploration and recreational canoeing were in their infancy and adventure tourism was something that virtually no one had yet thought of.

In the mid-1970s mineral exploration escalated enormously between Great Slave Lake and the Arctic Coast. Prospecting camps sprang up by the dozens and a seemingly endless parade of bush planes and helicopters blared overhead. By 1979 the search for minerals had become so intrusive that I withdrew my guiding operations from the entire western tundra region, and I never travelled west of the Thelon and Back river watersheds again. Over a period of just five years, the integrity of large areas of wilderness in the western Barren Lands had begun to erode.

The open boreal forest or taiga about fifty miles south of treeline. Most of the trees in this photograph are white spruce and the ground is covered with a thick carpet of lichen, the principal winter food of barren-ground caribou. After a forest fire, it requires forty to sixty years for lichens to re-establish themselves.

Looking across the breadth of the Thelon River near its headwater lakes (at the top of the photograph) with an esker and small lakes in the foreground.

A small lake on an esker, south-central Barren Lands.
PHOTO BY STUART MACKINNON.

Part of the Beverly caribou herd, mid July, Back River area of the Thelon Wildlife Sanctuary.

A tundra wolf on a sand dune, Thelon Wildlife Sanctuary.
PHOTO BY MONTE HUMMEL.

OPPOSITE

TOP: *A bull muskox, Thelon River.* PHOTO BY STAN HAMSTRA.

BOTTOM: *A curious tundra wolf approaches Carolyn Pritchett (early June, central Barrens).* PHOTO BY JAY PRITCHETT.

A small lake on an esker in the southern Barrens, Thelon River system.

The author and his wife Lia in the south-central Barren Lands, 1987.

Looking out over a sand dune beside the Thelon River on a mid-August evening. PHOTO BY ROCKY MONTGOMERY.

Looking out over a small, unnamed tundra river in the central Barren Lands (late June).

Since the 1970s wilderness has continued to deteriorate in this region as a result of increasing mining activity. The last two decades have also seen a proliferation of fishing, hunting and naturalist camps and lodges on the tundra north of Great Slave Lake and, to a lesser extent, north of Manitoba. Today, the Thelon and Back rivers and their tributaries are the only major watersheds north of treeline that are still relatively free of this kind of mining and tourism infrastructure and development.

The 1980s and '90s also witnessed tremendous growth in recreational canoeing across the Barren Lands. The nature of canoe trips changed as well. In the 1970s, trips of less than a month were almost unheard of, but by the 1980s, trips of two or three weeks had become the norm. Canoeists who flew into popular tundra rivers such as the Coppermine, Horton, Hood, Burnside, Thelon and Kazan were becoming a major source of revenue for northern air charter companies. Nowadays, many hundreds of wilderness enthusiasts can be found paddling these rivers in July and August, with even more pouring into the South Nahanni and other MacKenzie Mountain rivers farther west. With ever increasing numbers of canoeists being attracted from Europe as well as North America, the Northwest Territories and Nunavut have acquired an international reputation as the home of the best wilderness canoeing rivers left on earth.

By the late 1990s my retreat into the last truly unspoiled regions of the central Barren Lands was complete. Between 1992 and 1997 I gradually withdrew my early and late season canoe trips from the great tract of boreal forest lying north of Saskatchewan and southeast of Great Slave Lake. The reason for my retreat was wildfire.

Well into the 1970s, these jackpine and spruce-lichen woodlands were highly prized as vital winter caribou range, and the government actively protected them from lightning fires. But the climate of the boreal forest has warmed in recent decades, which has sparked more wildfires and longer fire seasons. From 1979 onwards, forest fires raged across the whole region southeast of Great Slave Lake, mostly unchecked. Some fires burned all summer and consumed tens of thousands of square miles of forest.

When I first travelled into this forest region in the 1970s, nearly all of it was green. By the mid-1990s most of it had been burned. Burnt forests are lost to caribou for forty to sixty years because it takes that long for lichen, their principal winter food, to reappear. They are lost to people like me for even longer because at these latitudes forests take so long to recover. As far as I'm concerned, one-hundred-year-old forests within one hundred miles of treeline are still uninviting scrublands. Warmer summers with their more frequent forest fires certainly don't augur well for the future of caribou populations or the recreational use of the boreal forest.

Some of the other physical changes that I have noticed since the 1970s have been less obvious. One of the most subtle has been a deterioration in the clarity of the air in the Barren Lands. Of course, this varies from summer to summer depending upon the frequency and size of forest fires in the general region. However, in the long run, I don't think the horizons are as sharp as they once were. While horizons in the Barren Lands are still much less hazy than those of the more densely populated parts of southern Canada, it wasn't so very long ago that you could see across the tundra for what felt like forever. This arctic haze is the result of airborne pollutants riding the air currents for thousands of miles from industrialized areas in Russia and Europe as well as North America.

I have also noticed subtle changes in the water. It seems to me that these days I hardly ever see the beautiful, vivid bands of blue and green I used to see so often in the clear waters of the rivers and lakes, especially over sandy bottoms. Again, this may be related to the clarity of the air or water, or both, as affected by global air pollution. With these subtle changes, the Barren Lands just don't seem as pristine to me as they once were.

One of the most disturbing changes I've seen in my travels has been a decline in the numbers of songbirds in the northernmost parts of the boreal forest. During the 1970s there used to be such cacophony of spring birdsongs through the twilight hours that pass for night at those latitudes that I sometimes had trouble sleeping. But by the 1990s I often experienced minutes of silence between birds singing in those same forests. In a matter of a decade or two, forests once vibrant with life had been transformed into lonely woods. These population declines are probably linked to habitat destruction in the birds' winter ranges in Mexico and in Central and South America.

In 1999 I co-authored a scientific paper that documented a northward expansion in the ranges of a number of birds and mammals from the boreal forest into the Barren Lands. Since 1970 at least three species of mammals (moose, otter and red squirrel) and more than a dozen species of birds have extended their breeding ranges as much as 230 miles north of treeline down the wooded valley of the Thelon River into the very heart of the tundra. Some of these birds include yellow-rumped warbler, rusty blackbird, lesser yellowlegs, Bonaparte's gull, bald eagle and a number of species of ducks, such as mallard, green-winged teal, widgeon, common merganser and lesser scaup. These northward range expansions may be explained by a warming of the climate beginning around 1970.

The very first mammalian invader from the boreal forest that I ever took note of in the Barren Lands was the moose. Since the 1970s, moose have expanded their range into all those parts of the southern and western Barrens where there are significant scattered pockets of spruce forest. The most remarkable increases in moose populations have occurred in the Thelon Oasis, where an abundance of willow results in some of the most productive moose habitat to be found in the North.

In the 1830s, when Captain George Back of the British Navy was embarking on his exploration of what is now known as the Back River, the Dene at Great Slave Lake told him that moose were present along the Thelon River. That population had disappeared by the end of the nineteenth century, when the Thelon was finally explored by David Hanbury and J.W. Tyrrell, and there was no sign of moose again on the Thelon before the 1950s.

The first moose seen on the Thelon in the twentieth century may have been a bull I saw on the upper river in 1973 and another deep in the oasis near Lookout Point in 1974. By 1977 I was seeing a lot of moose in the oasis and in 1992, my best year, I saw nineteen moose there in as many days. By then, there were obviously many hundreds of moose along the Thelon.

Barren-ground grizzlies have also increased substantially in recent years. In 1771 Samuel Hearne failed to see a single grizzly when he was guided across the Barren Lands and back by the Chipewyan leader, Matonabbee, although the Dene spoke of the presence of these bears in the northwestern tundra at the time and Hearne saw signs of them there. The Canadian Wildlife Service biologists who were studying barren-ground caribou in the 1950s and '60s believed grizzly populations began to grow in the central and eastern Barrens around 1950.

Barren-ground grizzly numbers have certainly increased dramatically since the days of Hearne and Matonabbee, and in my opinion most of that increase has taken place since 1970. I spent six summers on the Barrens in the 1970s and travelled widely before I saw my first grizzly. Since then, I have seen between one and eleven per summer, with an average of three to four. By the year 2000 I was seeing more grizzlies in a single summer than I saw throughout the 1970s. Grizzlies are now found almost everywhere on the mainland tundra, but there is a marked decrease in their numbers from west to east. They are also less abundant in the southernmost parts of the Barrens.

To understand some of the striking changes that have occurred in muskox populations in recent decades, we have to go back in history. In the eighteenth century, muskoxen ranged throughout the Barren Lands and south of treeline to some extent. Beginning about 1820, the Caribou Inuit began expanding their territory inland west of Hudson Bay, which put new pressures on the muskox population in that region. Also, a lucrative market in muskox robes opened up with the demise of the buffalo on the Great Plains in the 1880s. As a result, muskoxen were almost exterminated in the eastern Barrens by the Inuit, chiefly for food, and their numbers were greatly reduced in the western and central Barrens by Dene hunters, who slaughtered them for the robe trade. By 1917, when they were protected by law, muskoxen survived in no more than a half dozen of the most remote parts of the Barren Lands, perhaps most significantly in the vicinity of the Thelon Oasis. By then, there were thought to be only a few hundred muskoxen left on the Canadian mainland.

Mainland muskox populations were so low in the early twentieth century that several decades passed before there was any noticeable recovery. But then the momentum began to build. In the 1960s and '70s, for example, muskox numbers began to grow rapidly in the Queen Maud Gulf area north of the Thelon Wildlife Sanctuary. Then, in the 1980s, muskoxen began to recolonize tundra areas west, south and east of the sanctuary. Throughout the 1980s and '90s I saw muskoxen reoccupy huge areas of the southern Barrens as far as treeline and beyond into the boreal forest in some locations. By the year 2000, muskoxen could be found throughout the entire upper Thelon River drainage system. One of the great thrills of my life has been the realization that muskoxen were going to reoccupy large areas of the southern Barrens in my lifetime, and then watching that happen even sooner than I thought possible. Today, almost the only parts of their former range that muskoxen have yet to recolonize are the most eastern areas towards Hudson Bay.

At the same time as they were expanding their range to the south, muskoxen were declining in the older core areas such as the Thelon Wildlife Sanctuary, the vicinity of Bathurst Inlet and south of Queen Maud Gulf. By the late 1990s my clients and I were seeing as few as one or two muskoxen on our canoe trips in the Thelon Oasis. Previous to this, muskox sightings along the middle Thelon River were virtually an everyday occurrence. We often saw many dozens in a single day.

The largest number of muskoxen that I ever encountered in the Thelon sanctuary was in 1992 when I saw 464 within a five-week period. In 1993 I saw only 153 muskoxen in the sanctuary during the same five weeks, then thirty in 1997 and just six in 1999. Obviously, there was a precipitous decline in muskox numbers in the sanctuary after 1992. Although I have no evidence that could explain the cause, I have two possible clues. One is that herd sizes became much smaller after 1992 and the other is that I have never seen many calves or yearlings in any of the sanctuary herds. By contrast, the herds south of the sanctuary, where the population was expanding during the 1980s and '90s, always contained large numbers of young animals. The possibilities for this decline range from large-scale movements to large-scale die-offs or grizzly bear predation on calves. In my opinion, the latter factor deserves considerable scrutiny.

The muskox may seem like the quintessential tundra mammal, but in many more important ways the Barren Lands are the land of the caribou. Even so, several of the largest caribou herds usually leave the tundra for most of the winter and migrate into the boreal forest, where they are subject to much more intensive hunting pressure. Thousands of tundra wolves follow the caribou on their winter migrations wherever they go. It is during the winter, when these wolves are often highly concentrated among large aggregations of caribou, that these big predators are most susceptible to hunting or more insidious forms of control by man.

During the so-called "caribou crisis" of the 1950s, biologists were convinced that over-hunting by Dene and Inuit had reduced barren-ground caribou populations from over two million animals to some 200,000 in the previous half century. To help stem the tide, a wolf control program was initiated on the winter ranges of the three major caribou herds. For six consecutive years, over 1,500 tundra wolves were poisoned each winter. The eleven-year program was considered a success when it began to wind down in 1962, as the number of wolves that were killed had decreased substantially during 1959–62, despite no let-up in the poisoning effort.

The biologists also found the age structure of the wolf population had changed from a low of 13 percent full-grown pups early in the poisoning campaign to 73 percent by the winter of 1960–61. Wolves have a high potential rate of increase, but under normal conditions, when populations are relatively stable, that potential is never realized. Most pups die at an early age. This was the case when the poisoning program began. However, wolf populations can sustain mortality rates well in excess of 50 percent of their numbers. By the end of the poisoning campaign, when wolf populations were clearly in decline, pup production had probably increased and pup survival had obviously mushroomed to compensate for the heavy mortality.

After the poisoning program was curbed in the early 1960s, wolf populations undoubtedly rebounded to their former levels within several years. Throughout the 1970s and '80s I typically saw between twenty-five and forty-five tundra wolves each summer on my canoe trips. My best summer was 1992, when I saw fifty-seven. Those numbers dropped off after 1992; by 1996 and 1997 I was seeing only ten wolves each summer. Similarly, the number of active wolf dens with pups that I encountered fell from nine in 1992 to zero in 1997. Typically, I visit close to twenty wolf dens per summer.

My annual wolf sightings suggested wolf numbers were decreasing in the 1990s on the range of the Beverly caribou herd, but I had no idea why until February of 1998. That was when the *Globe and Mail* ran a story exposing the extent of that winter's wolf kill in a treeline area around the southeastern headwaters of the Thelon River and south into the taiga. Some more digging on my part revealed that a handful of Dene hunters based out of northern Saskatchewan had been killing up to seven hundred wolves each winter throughout the 1990s in this relatively small area. The pelts commanded higher prices than any other furbearer on the market. Most were sold for rug mounts.

Nearly all of these wolves were shot at very close range after being overtaken on the smooth surfaces of frozen lakes by high-powered snowmobiles. With the illegal use of caribou carcasses as bait, at least some of the hunters were luring wolves far out onto the ice of big lakes, where they were much more vulnerable than on land. Using these methods, these hunters were wiping out entire wolf packs. Running down wildlife with snowmobiles was illegal in every jurisdiction of Canada except the Northwest Territories.

The wolf kills by these Dene hunters were greatest during those winters, when caribou, and the wolves associated with them, were highly concentrated in the hunters' particular area. The wolf poisoning campaign of the 1950s, which covered a huge area, targeted the wolves that preyed upon the three major caribou herds. The wolf kills by the Saskatchewan hunters in the 1990s, on the other hand, were largely limited to the wolves associated with the Beverly caribou herd. Nevertheless, movements of wolves and caribou fitted with satellite collars indicated that the Saskatchewan hunters were also taking wolves attached to the Bathurst and Ahiak caribou herds in some of those years.

Did these Dene hunters kill enough wolves to decrease the wolf population associated with the Beverly herd? That's a difficult question to answer without knowing the size of this wolf population to begin with. I'm sceptical that the human kill was large enough on its own to have a dramatic effect on wolf numbers, although it certainly would have been an important contributing factor if some other cause was also at work. It is noteworthy, however, that over the past several years the price for wolf pelts has fallen and the numbers of wolves killed by these aboriginal hunters has dropped substantially. Correspondingly, the number of wolves sighted on our canoe trips increased to thirty-six in 2001, and the number of active dens we encountered rose to eight.

After the wolf poisoning program was cut back in 1962, wildlife biologists measured significant increases in the caribou population over the next eight or nine years. All of the information the biologists had collected had indicated that caribou were being over-hunted by man, but by reducing the wolf population in the 1950s and early

'60s, these scientists thought they had provided caribou populations with a foothold towards recovery. Nevertheless, aerial censuses indicated that caribou numbers declined throughout the 1970s; the biologists were convinced that overhunting by aboriginal people was the cause. By 1980 caribou biologists believed there were only about 250,000 caribou left in the three major herds and less than 400,000 in all of the Barren Lands.

By 1978 it was obvious to me that the official estimates of caribou populations were far too low, because on my annual canoe trips I had seen single aggregations of caribou containing as many as 200,000 animals. Others had come to the same conclusion I had, including Inuit hunters along the Hudson Bay Coast. When I shared my observations with the government biologists in Yellowknife, not only was I not believed, I was ridiculed.

All this began to change when my friend Cormack Gates became the regional biologist for the Keewatin District, adjacent to Hudson Bay. In 1982 Cormack conducted an aerial survey of the Qamanirjuaq herd in the Keewatin and estimated it at 133,000 caribou. Since the previous estimate, just two years earlier, had been 39,000, Cormack's superiors in Yellowknife accused him of committing major mistakes in his survey methods, and he was instructed to repeat the census the next year. However, Cormack came up with a similar estimate again in 1983. Obviously, there were a lot more caribou in the southern Keewatin than was commonly acknowledged in government circles.

In the early 1980s government biologists began to experiment with a new method of censusing caribou that involved counting animals on air photographs. When this method replaced the old technique of visual counts from aircraft, estimates of caribou numbers skyrocketed. By the year 2001, Anne Gunn, the current caribou biologist, estimated that caribou populations in the Barren Lands totalled some 1.3 million animals (excluding calves) in four major herds, with another 250,000 in a dozen minor herds.

Although there has been a great deal of confusion about caribou numbers, almost everyone would agree that there have been increases since the days of the "caribou crisis" in the 1950s. Increases, yes—but by how much is difficult to say because the old techniques of censusing caribou were highly inaccurate and greatly underestimated the actual population. Today, more is also known about the caribou herds that occupy the northernmost parts of the Barren Lands. For example, only a few decades ago, the Ahiak herd was thought to be insignificant, but now it has been elevated to the status of a major herd.

More obvious than the changes in caribou numbers are the recent increases in muskox, moose, grizzly and wolverine populations and the impact of global warming on wildlife in northern latitudes. But of all the changes that have taken place over the past half century, none is more significant than the fact that we have moved steadily away from the old North, where small groups of aboriginal hunters and trappers were still scattered thinly over the land, and into an era where the relentless grasp of industrialization is beginning to reach into the innermost recesses of the Barren Lands. And with the beginning of industrialization, huge areas of wilderness are about to be sacrificed.

The Battle for the Thelon

The election of a Progressive Conservative government to power in Ottawa in 1984 under Brian Mulroney ushered in sweeping changes that, among other things, threatened the viability of critical wildlife areas across northern Canada. This first became apparent in December 1986, when the Minister of Indian Affairs and Northern Development released his Northern Mineral Policy declaring his government's commitment to "maximizing the land area available for mineral exploration and development while ensuring that unique and representative natural features of land, cultural and wildlife resources are protected." In addition to reviewing the boundaries of bird sanctuaries and the disposition of 116 International Biological Program sites in the Northwest Territories, the minister stated that "in consultation with aboriginal associations, the federal and territorial governments will review resource utilization in the Thelon Game Sanctuary with the objective of ensuring the widest range of activities compatible with the original goal of muskox protection." With these words, the minister not only demonstrated his bias in favour of the mining industry, but clearly indicated his government was championing the multiple-use philosophy that was in vogue with conservatives in the United States during those years. What it meant was that the mining industry was going to get pretty much what it wanted in the Thelon Game Sanctuary.

As early as 1956, the mining industry had convinced the federal government of the day to lop off a huge chunk from the western part of the sanctuary for mineral exploration. By 1981 much of the upper Thelon River and other areas to the east of the sanctuary had been staked for uranium, right up to the sanctuary's boundaries.

The mining industry believed the sanctuary was full of uranium, and it had been actively lobbying the federal government to open up, reduce or abolish the sanctuary since the 1970s. When Brian Mulroney's Conservatives voiced their intent to review the status and boundaries of the sanctuary in 1986, they signalled that they had bought into the mining lobby's propaganda that the Thelon was nothing more than a sixty-year-old muskox preserve that had long outlived its original purpose.

Although it was almost another year before this issue received much attention in the North or anywhere else in the nation, I was marshalling my forces to fight for the Thelon within days of the announcement of the new mineral policy. I have often wondered if I'd have had the strength of my convictions to wage this battle during that lonely first year had it not been for an incident that put me in the public limelight some months earlier. At that time, the Canadian government was considering a proposal to allow low-level military flights along a corridor that would begin over the western end of the Thelon Game Sanctuary and proceed south to the Canadian Forces base at Cold Lake, Alberta. These low-level training manoeuvres would include American B-52 bombers and Canadian CF-18 fighters at altitudes as low as 350 feet above ground level. The proposed flight line would pass right over some of the rivers I used in my guiding business. Since I was the only person in the Northwest Territories protesting these flights because my livelihood was at stake, I received a lot of attention from the press and CBC radio. To my complete surprise, the military moved the flight line farther west, closer to the communities, to accommodate me. With the Cold War winding down, the low-level flights never materialized, but that experience taught me a very valuable lesson: the North has a tiny population with few voices, and one voice can make a difference. During that lonely first year of the battle for the Thelon Game Sanctuary, I clung to the belief that my voice could have an impact and that there was always a chance of winning.

One of the first actions I took was to write to all the clients I had taken into the Thelon over the years. I warned them that the sanctuary was at risk and urged them to write the federal minister in charge of the Department of Indian Affairs and Northern Development (DIAND). They responded by the dozens from all over North America and from Europe and Australia with heartfelt letters about their Thelon experiences, imploring the minister to leave the sanctuary inviolate for future generations. I later learned that officials at DIAND were caught completely off guard by those letters. They were amazed that so many people from all over the world had even heard of this remote sanctuary, let alone had been there or cared about its future. And it never hurts when Americans proclaim the Thelon to be one of the great natural wonders of the world, unequalled by anything in their own country. In the fall of 1987 the minister of DIAND announced he would postpone his decision on the status of the Thelon for at least another year. This bought us some desperately needed time, and I like to think my clients' letters had a lot to do with that.

As it turned out, this battle kept me on the offensive for three years. I wrote hundreds of letters to politicians, newspapers, clients, southern-based conservation and canoeing organizations, a variety of northern organizations and the committee that was created to study the federal government's proposal. I sponsored resolutions on the Thelon for several national and territorial organizations and kept a network of organizations and individuals in southern Canada informed about the progress of the campaign in the North. During this period, I also became president of the NWT Wildlife Federation, which gave me another pulpit to preach from. I had a lot to say about the Thelon and DIAND, and I received a lot of publicity for it. At the same time, some of my southern Canadian clients were busy badgering their members of Parliament and their favourite environmental organizations about the plight of the sanctuary.

By December 1987 the future of the Thelon was becoming a motherhood issue in the North. Support for the sanctuary also grew rapidly in southern Canada in 1988, thanks to the efforts of several national conservation organizations. The cause even garnered some editorials in major newspapers. On the national scene, Paul Griss, executive director of the Canadian Nature Federation, was an early and particularly effective voice.

It may have taken a while, but in the end there was a huge public outcry, and DIAND was totally unprepared for it when it finally erupted. In the Northwest Territories, politicians and every organization that counted—aboriginal or otherwise—declared their support for maintaining the Thelon's status quo. Gordon Wray, Baker Lake's representative in the territorial legislature declared the federal government's review of the sanctuary "insensitive and outright stupid." Jim Bourque, the highly respected Deputy Minister of Renewable Resources, called for an expansion of the Thelon's boundaries. The mining industry was completely isolated on the issue and was seen as greedy for not being satisfied with the 95 percent of the NWT that was already available for mineral exploration and development.

With such overwhelming public support in the North, it was hardly surprising when, in June 1990, the federal government announced it was backing down. There would be no change to the Thelon's status or boundaries. The precious jewel the Thelon, the heart and soul of the Barren Lands, was safe, at least for a while. Victory was sweet, but there were also some consequences. The battle had brought a lot of publicity to the sanctuary, and I knew I would be seeing more people there.

On the Brink

In the late 1980s, when we were battling the federal government and the mining industry to save the Thelon, Urangesellschaft Canada was proposing a huge, open-pit uranium mine just east of the sanctuary. The Inuit in the communities along Hudson Bay, and in nearby Baker Lake in particular, opposed the mine and effectively blocked its construction. A collapse in the price of uranium in the early 1980s also slowed its exploration in the North. Of the eight companies exploring for uranium in the upper Thelon basin south of the sanctuary in 1981, only one remained by the mid-1980s. Today, one discovery of uranium in association with precious metals still remains viable on the upper Thelon River.

Further east near Hudson Bay, mineral exploration was becoming more intensive in the 1980s, especially for gold. One gold mine went into production just north of Manitoba during this period, but only briefly. The mining industry's greatest interest has always been in the richly mineralized western Barrens, where the Slave Geological Province stretches north from Great Slave Lake to Coronation Gulf on the Arctic Ocean. Exploration for precious and base metals accelerated on a grand scale in this region in the mid-1970s. In 1982 the Lupin Gold Mine began operations at the north end of Contwoyto Lake, with a winter ice-road supplying it from Yellowknife across the tundra. Then, to the surprise of almost everyone, diamonds were discovered in 1991 on the headwaters of the Coppermine River, two hundred miles northeast of Yellowknife. And with that ominous discovery, nothing in the Barren Lands would ever be the same again.

The discovery of diamonds meant the beginning of the end of the Barren Lands as our last great wilderness. Many of us realized that almost instantly. It didn't take much foresight to understand the sequence of events that would lead to full-scale mineral development in the Slave Geological Province. Many potential mines containing various kinds of metals had been discovered all over this region in recent years, but few of them would ever be economically viable until they were accessible by an all-weather road. Before the diamond discoveries, it looked like those potential mines were going to have to wait a long time for that all-weather road. But a multibillion-dollar diamond mine coming into production—or several of them, as it soon became clear—would change everything. The diamond mines would drive industrial development throughout the entire region. They would act as the catalyst that the mining industry needed to jump-start the construction of an all-weather road northeast from Yellowknife. That road, in turn, would act as a fuse that would lead to an explosion of other mines and roads over a huge area. In a matter of a few years, the entire western Barrens would be opened up to mining. Barrenland rivers would be dammed to power those mines, and hydroelectric transmission lines would radiate across the tundra.

The diamond discoveries in 1991 ignited the largest mining rush in Canadian history. Over the next four years, 260 companies staked 85,000 square miles of land, an area twice the size of the island of Newfoundland. As a result, millions of claim posts now litter an immense region of tundra.

By 1994 the Government of the Northwest Territories was planning an all-weather road through the mining discoveries, linking Yellowknife with a proposed deep-water port just east of Kugluktuk on the Arctic coast. The NWT Power Corporation also identified potential hydro-power sites that could be developed on the region's rivers. The money for this infrastructure was to come from the Government of Canada, but when the territorial government recommended the federal government "invest" $650 million in the all-weather road and port, Ottawa declined.

In 1998 the territorial government realigned its proposed all-season road to terminate at a potential deep-water port at the south end of Bathurst Inlet, passing through part of the Bathurst caribou herd's calving grounds just west of the inlet. The road would begin at Rae-Edzo or Yellowknife and would cover a distance of between 450 and 520 miles. The southern part of the road as far as the Izok Lake discovery—one of the largest undeveloped lead–zinc–copper deposits in North America—would cost between $380 and $430 million. However, construction of the northern part of the road from Izok Lake to Bathurst Inlet, together with the port, would cost only $180 million. Until just before this book went to press, it appeared that the northern part of the road would be built within the next few years, pending an environmental review. Construction of the deep-water port facility at Bathurst Inlet, followed by a 175-mile, year-round road from the coast into the mineral-rich interior as far as Izok Lake, was scheduled to begin in 2004. But the price of lead-zinc has fallen, and the development of the Izok Lake mine has been put on hold. As a result, the Bathurst Inlet port and road project has been delayed for at least another year.

As part of the land claim settlement between the Inuit and the federal government, the new territory of Nunavut was carved out of the old Northwest Territories in 1999. As a result, most of the Barren Lands are now within the political boundaries of Nunavut. The Inuit will benefit financially from mining activity in Nunavut as part of the terms of their land claim agreement. And they have made it clear to the mining industry that they are open for business. Not only does the land claim provide the Inuit with royalties from mineral development, it also requires mining companies to negotiate Impact and Benefit Agreements with the Inuit before operating in Nunavut. These agreements promise the Inuit financial compensation, education, business contracts and construction and mining jobs. As well, the Inuit now own 18 percent (137,450 square miles) of the land in Nunavut, including the mineral rights to 14,628 square miles of that land. Understandably, many view Impact and Benefit Agreements as nothing more than thinly veiled bribes.

In recent decades, the Inuit have been moving away from the old hunting way of life on the land into a wage economy. With Nunavut's huge unemployment rate (over 30 percent) and a birth rate that is twice the national average, many Inuit leaders, and increasingly the population in general, are now looking to the mining industry to solve their chronic unemployment problems. Many politicians in Nunavut see roads to resources as a key part of that solution. As a result, a number of influential Inuit have been actively promoting the Bathurst Inlet port and road proposal, which fell within the jurisdiction of Nunavut in 1999. Also, in February 2000, the premiers of Nunavut and Manitoba signed an agreement to pursue their common goal of connecting the southern Nunavut mining discoveries and the Inuit communities along Hudson Bay with the rest of Canada via a $2 to $3 billion all-weather road through northern Manitoba.

At present there are just three operating mines in the Barren Lands—the Lupin Gold Mine at Contwoyto Lake and two diamond mines at Lac de Gras (BHP's Ekati Mine and the Diavik Mine). At least two more diamond mines on the tundra northeast of Yellowknife are also in the planning stages. And new diamond

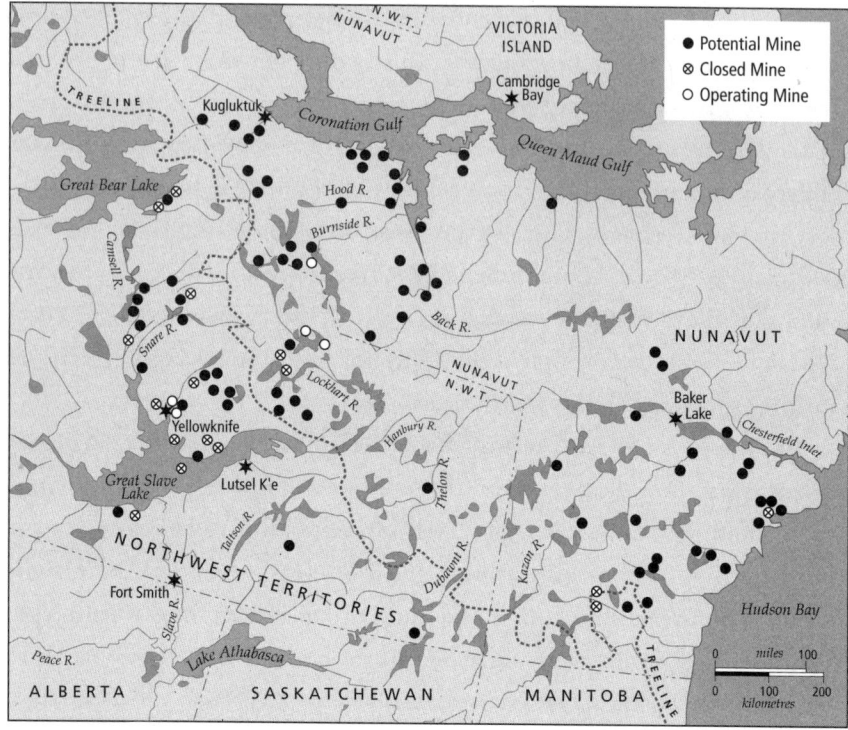

discoveries are still taking place. As this book goes to press, the large staking rush for diamonds that began in the winter of 2002 is continuing in Nunavut between Contwoyto Lake and Kugluktuk.

More important, at least another sixty potential mines of various kinds have been discovered in the Barren Lands to date. Some of these would probably be operating mines today had it not been for a slump in gold prices that began in 1996. Of these sixty potential mines, twenty-four are located in the Slave Geological Province and over half of those are gold deposits, many of which surround Bathurst Inlet. Another twenty are gold, uranium, base metal and diamond discoveries in the area south of Baker Lake and Chesterfield Inlet near Hudson Bay. With dozens of mines now waiting in the wings, the southeastern corner and much of the western half of the Barren Lands are poised on the brink of industrial development.

By the mid-1990s diamond fever was rampant within the nation's media. There was no end to the glowing stories in newspapers and magazines about the romance of finding diamonds in Canada's North and the riches they would bestow. But only once did I ever read a story that dealt with the value of the Barren Lands beyond that of its mineral resources. Only once did any of these journalists ever consider how the diamond discoveries might lead to the industrialization of one of the largest wildernesses left on earth. Then too, the mining industry, it seemed, never missed an opportunity to prey upon the ignorance of the public and the press by portraying the Barren Lands as a virtual wasteland, good for nothing but mineral extraction. Here, for example, are the opening sentences in one mining company's brochure aimed at investors for its diamond explorations: "The tundra of Canada's Northwest Territories, just below the Arctic Circle, supports little more than an occasional grizzly or migrating caribou. In the perpetual twilight of winter, glacier scarred rock, ice and snow dominate a landscape visited by temperatures as low as minus seventy degrees centigrade. The region is, however, one of the earth's most bountiful, yielding up copper, silver and gold."

When diamonds were discovered in 1991, I was gripped by the awful certainty that wilderness, as I knew it, would be destroyed in most of the western half of the Barren Lands within the next twenty-five years. Many still doubt such a transformation will happen so quickly and dismiss people like me as mere "naysayers." To them, a few mines in the vastness of the Barren Lands have no more significance than a few pinpricks on a very large map. But I can't help remembering what happened to the Great Plains in the nineteenth century. During the age of the horse and the steam-powered locomotive, that wilderness, along with its millions of buffalo and its way of life, completely vanished within a forty-year period, well within one person's lifetime. The beginning of the twenty-first century in the Barren Lands is probably the equivalent of the 1860s on the Great Plains. We are at a turning point in history. The days of the big, northern wilderness are fast coming to an end.

In 1996, before Canada's first diamond mine—the BHP mine at Lac de Gras—could receive approval to begin operations, it was subjected to a federal environmental assessment review, with public hearings held in Yellowknife. Stopping a diamond mine would be virtually impossible, but this wasn't the time to accept defeat. It was a time to stand up and be counted. I wanted to tell the public what the Barren Lands mean to me, what I think they should mean for all Canadians and how the development of diamond mines would lead to the decimation of large areas of northern wilderness. In my view, this was a historic moment and I felt compelled to make my feelings known in both a written submission and through an oral presentation in Yellowknife. Below is most of a letter I wrote in April 1995 to the panel that was struck to conduct the environmental assessment.

> ...If the BHP diamond mine becomes a reality at Lac de Gras...it is almost certain to trigger a chain of events that will soon destroy a substantial part of the largest wilderness left in Canada. Although BHP's proposal does not include an all-weather road connecting its mine with Yellowknife, only the naive believe such a road will never be built. The territorial government, it seems, is fairly slavering at the mouth over the prospects of diamond mines and an all-weather road to open up mining of all kinds throughout the whole region north of Great Slave Lake. A diamond mine at Lac de Gras will be more grist

for the mill of the formidable forces now lobbying for an all-weather road deep into the Barren Lands...

Roads always breed more roads. In this case, an all-weather road would mean more mines, hydroelectric dams and more roads as far north as the Arctic coast. Much of the western half of the Barren Lands would soon be cut up by roads, or "developed," as they call it. The trucks, bulldozers, miners, entrepreneurs and tourists will come by the thousands, but the great, wild land will be gone from the Great Slave Lake north to the shores of the Arctic Ocean.

How much longer will the eastern Barrens last? Can it be long before an all-weather road is built from Churchill up the west coast of Hudson Bay to Rankin Inlet and beyond? Most will say we'll be richer for these mines and roads but, in my opinion, we'll be poorer. The Barren Lands of the Northwest Territories are the last great stronghold of virgin wildlands left on the North American continent. Chances are very real that most of this vast wilderness will disappear in our own lifetimes. It will all be carved up into smaller pieces for its mineral wealth and for the almighty, short-term dollar. The real tragedy is that mines don't last forever, but once the roads are built the wilderness is gone forever.

Look what we've done to this Garden of Eden of a continent of ours in the past four hundred years. We've heaped destruction on the original inhabitants and their land as they knew it. We've overrun North America in our hundreds of millions. We've turned almost every part of this continent that we can into croplands to feed those millions. We've cut down the forests, polluted the rivers and paved over too much of the rest. Today, there isn't a single location in the United States, south of

Alaska, that is farther than twenty-one miles from a road. Would any Huron or Iroquois from three hundred years ago recognize anything of his or her homeland in present day southern Ontario or New York State? Would any wandering Plains Cree hunter from 150 years ago recognize anything of the former buffalo prairies of the Saskatchewan today?

The Barren Lands and northern fringes of the boreal forest within the Northwest Territories are the last major part of the North American continent that is still much as it was when the white man first arrived. Matonabbee, the great Chipewyan leader who guided Samuel Hearne across thousands of miles of that land in the 1770s, would still recognize virtually all of his old haunts today, from Hudson Bay west to Great Slave Lake and north to the Arctic Ocean. Even here, profound changes have occurred since Matonabbee's day. Most of this land is now uninhabited; the huge, migratory caribou herds are diminished and only in recent decades have muskox populations begun to rebound after near extinction in the nineteenth century. However, the land itself is still the same, still in its original, pristine, natural state.

It seems that is all going to change very soon. Some will say that's progress; the world's few remaining wild places must be tamed and their riches extracted. It will mean more money and jobs. Perhaps it's inevitable, only a matter of time. But didn't we learn any lessons farther south over the past four hundred years? Are we going to make all the same old mistakes again in the North in the dawning of the twenty-first century? It seems that we are and that North America's last great wilderness will soon be gone. Few may mourn its passing because so very few have ever had the privilege of knowing it.

I know that country where they're searching for diamonds. I know what it was like before the geologists, claim-stakers, helicopters and trucks on winter roads swarmed over it. I know what it was like to roam across that virgin land for hundreds of miles, as free as the caribou, and to never see another soul or sign of modern man for weeks on end.

Twenty years ago, when I was still a young man, I realized that the giant, unspoiled wilderness of the Barren Lands could easily disappear in my own lifetime. From the mid-1970s to the early 1980s I worried as mineral exploration heated up. Then it cooled down. Now we appear to be on the brink of losing it all, with the discovery of diamonds. I only hope my ashes will be laid to rest along my favourite rivers before the last of that big, wild country disappears forever. As for future generations of Canadians, they'll have to settle for the bits and pieces that are left over. And when the great, open, wild spaces are gone, what will happen to the caribou, who can say.

In February, 1996, I briefly addressed the environmental assessment panel in Yellowknife. Below are some of my comments.

...The migratory caribou herds, especially the Bathurst herd, could also be at risk. There's something mystical and unpredictable about caribou. They seem to need large wilderness areas to prosper. Wilderness areas required by barren-ground caribou are large indeed, what with single herds now approaching one-half million animals and annual migrations that range over hundreds of miles of territory. No one can predict with any certainty what will happen to caribou populations as the wilderness shrinks, but I don't think that anyone who knows much about caribou could be optimistic about their future over the next fifty or one hundred years...

You panel members will be hearing from a lot of people who are thinking only of their bank accounts and who don't give a damn about what happens to that country out there as long as it makes money for them. You will also be hearing from a lot of people who think they can have the money and jobs these mines will bring and protect the land at the same time. No doubt, this is the approach you panel members will eventually recommend we try to take. But modern history, and especially North American history, has shown us that this approach is terribly naive. You simply can't have it both ways. Realists will agree that bringing this diamond mine into production will launch us down a slippery slope from which there may be no turning back before a network of roads, mines, hydroelectric dams and transmission lines covers much of the Barren Lands...

The sheer size of the continental Barrens of the Northwest Territories makes them a wilderness of global importance. The Barren Lands are a national treasure that must not be looted without the consent of the citizens of Canada. It is vital to our national interest that we recognize how these proposed diamond mines are likely to lead to the fragmentation and degradation of a wilderness that comprises one-eighth of our nation...All Canadians, but especially Northerners, and most especially aboriginal Northerners, must understand that we are already at the crossroads where we must decide whether we want to keep our country's largest wilderness or give it up to the mining industry...

If the Barren Lands were mine to sell I wouldn't sell them for all the diamonds and gold on the face of this earth. I would gladly give my life to keep them wild forever. That's what the Barren Lands mean to me. But then, you'd have to live and travel for some time in that country out there before you could understand what I'm talking about. My children may never have the opportunity to know the Barren Lands in the same way that I have, but for my grandchildren, I'm afraid, there may only be fragments of the vast wilderness I knew.

There's no doubt in my mind, and I don't think there's much doubt in anybody else's, as to what road we're going to be heading down with regards to these diamond mines. It's that same old road of exploitation we've been heading down for the last four hundred years and the next victim will be the largest wilderness left on this continent. Money and greed will prevail as they nearly always do.

But in the process we'll be losing something valuable. And it's something that's not all that tangible or easy to evaluate. But it's something that's an important part of what defines this country of ours and helps to make it distinct from the United States and from the rest of the world. And it's something that's part of what shapes us and makes us what we are as a people.

And when our last great wilderness is carved up by roads to mines and its rivers dammed to provide power for those mines, I ask you: will we be richer or will we be poorer? And what will it tell us about what kind of a country Canada is? What will it tell us about what kind of a people we are? Some of us, I know, are going to be a lot less proud to call ourselves Canadians.

The Vision

David Pelly and I first met on the Thelon River in July 1992. David was in the process of writing his book *Thelon: A River Sanctuary*, and he and his wife, Laurie, had prearranged to meet a group of my clients and me at Warden's Grove, then accompany us for four days of our canoe trip. That was the beginning of an unusual friendship that has lasted to this day. What's unusual about it is that, apart from another brief meeting in 1992, David and I have never seen each other again; but there's hardly a month or even a week in the year when we aren't writing or talking to each other about some issue of mutual interest connected with the Barren Lands.

By the early 1990s, David and I knew full well that the best hope for wilderness on the mainland tundra lay in the central region, where there was no longer much interest on the part of the mining industry after the collapse of the price of uranium ten years earlier. Some 45,000 square miles of this region were already protected to some degree by the Thelon Wildlife Sanctuary and the Queen Maud Gulf Migratory Bird Sanctuary. As a bird sanctuary, however, the Queen Maud cannot be considered a bona fide protected area because it can only protect birds, not their habitat. But in the mid-1990s, the Canadian Wildlife Service, with the support of the pre-implemented Nunavut Wildlife Management Board, wanted to upgrade the Queen Maud to a National Wildlife Area, which would better protect it from mineral exploration and development. The wildlife management board's support was contingent upon the wildlife service obtaining approvals for its initiative from local and regional interests. However, the wildlife service never proceeded with the necessary community consultations, and the whole process has been stalled indefinitely for insufficient political support in Nunavut and inadequate financial commitments to the cause by the wildlife service. Under its present status, the Queen Maud can only be explored for minerals with the consent of the Nunavut Wildlife Management Board and the Canadian Wildlife Service, both of which have previously opposed mineral exploration in this sanctuary.

The Queen Maud Gulf Migratory Bird Sanctuary was created in 1961 to protect one of the largest concentrations of geese on earth. Today, there is a breeding population of well over two million geese in this 24,000-square-mile sanctuary. The Queen Maud is the most important breeding area in North America for white-fronted geese, contains the nesting grounds of 95 percent of the world population of Ross's geese, and has one of the world's major concentrations of snow geese, as well as thousands of Canada geese, brant, tundra swans and sandhill cranes. In 1982, the United Nations designated this sanctuary a "Wetland of International Importance" under the terms of the Ramsar Convention.

In order to protect such globally significant waterfowl habitat, Queen Maud uniquely contains 180 miles of arctic coastline, giving the sanctuary an important marine component. The inland portion is a vast, gently rolling lowland of Canadian Shield drained by several northward-flowing rivers. The sanctuary is spattered with countless ponds and shallow lakes, which are surrounded by expanses of wet sedge meadows and lush tundra. These are also crucial breeding grounds for hundreds of thousands of shorebirds, such as pectoral sandpipers, semipalmated sandpipers and lesser golden plovers.

The Queen Maud sanctuary includes the majority of the calving grounds of the 200,000 caribou of the Ahiak herd, which migrate into the Thelon sanctuary and upper Thelon River area as far south as the treeline for the winter. Traditionally, the Queen Maud sanctuary also contained the eastern part of the calving grounds of the 350,000-strong Bathurst caribou herd, but since 1990 this herd has calved west of the sanctuary. Queen Maud also has some four thousand muskoxen, including rare blond animals not known to occur elsewhere.

With the threat of industrialization of the Barren Lands becoming so imminent by the mid-1990s, David Pelly and I were becoming much more aware of the significance of the fact that the most pristine, uninhabited areas and the most important wildlife areas were to be found in the central Barrens. It was also apparent that the mining industry's current interests lay in regions further east and west and that with the Nunavut land claim settled, there would never be much aboriginal-owned land in the central Barrens. Given this unique combination of circumstances and the fact that the Thelon and Queen Maud sanctuaries are only forty-five miles apart, David and I decided that we should begin promoting the idea of linking the two sanctuaries together. One attractive feature of our proposal was that it could protect the remainder of the calving grounds of the Beverly caribou herd that lay outside the Thelon Wildlife Sanctuary.

Even though the Thelon is the largest protected area in Canada today, it can't even come close to protecting the populations of most of its large mammals. The migratory patterns of the half-million caribou of the Beverly and Ahiak herds mean that they spend only part of the year in this sanctuary, as do the tundra wolves and wolverines that follow them. Even barren-ground grizzlies can range over two hundred miles or more of tundra. Conservation biologists worldwide agree that the most serious constraint in establishing conservation reserves today is making them big enough to be truly self-sufficient—in other words, ensuring that they are places where the forces of nature are permitted to function freely to maintain population viability and habitat diversity in the face of environmental change. Joining the Thelon and Queen Maud sanctuaries together still wouldn't protect an area large enough to encompass the home ranges of caribou, wolves and wolverines, or even a large number of grizzly bears, but it would certainly preserve critical habitat in the form of calving grounds and denning areas.

With the border of the new territory of Nunavut cutting through the heart of the Thelon Wildlife Sanctuary, 60 percent of the sanctuary became part of Nunavut in 1999. The terms of the Nunavut land claim settlement required the territorial government to coordinate the preparation of a management plan for the sanctuary, to be finalized and approved before division of the old NWT into two new territories. To that end, the Akiliniq Planning Committee, comprising primarily Inuit in Nunavut, was established in 1994, along with a parallel committee made up of Dene from Lutsel K'e representing the NWT portion of the sanctuary. In a spirit of cooperation, the Inuit and Dene met in the sanctuary in August of 1995 and signed a statement pledging to develop a management plan for the preservation of the sanctuary that would be sensitive to the needs, wishes and rights of both peoples. In November of 1995, the Lutsel K'e Dene disbanded their committee in favour of establishing a more broadly based land use planning effort related to their Treaty Entitlement process. Nevertheless, the Dene continued to participate on an observer basis with the Akiliniq Planning Committee based in Baker Lake. In 1996, the planning committee tabled a draft management plan for the sanctuary that, in effect, represented the collaborative efforts and shared conservation vision of the Inuit and Dene.

As part of the process of creating a management plan for the sanctuary, the Akiliniq Planning Committee invited the public to participate at several stages in the plan's development. David Pelly and I took full advantage of this invitation and were successful in convincing the planning committee to adopt a number of our suggestions. Although we didn't think the committee would or could act on the subject of boundary changes, David and I both proposed an expansion of the sanctuary to the northeast to include all of the calving grounds of the Beverly caribou herd. I also argued for a boundary expansion to the southwest to include the upper Thelon River. In particular, I proposed a thirty-five-mile extension of the sanctuary along the Thelon valley south of Eyeberry Lake. Such an extension would return an area to the protection of the sanctuary that was excised in 1956, an area extremely rich in wildlife and boreal vegetation. In fact, the entire upper Thelon watershed is rich in wildlife, comparable to the sanctuary itself in both its variety of species and its populations. It contains the major migration routes of the Beverly and Ahiak caribou herds, and by the mid-1990s it had larger populations of muskoxen than occurred inside the sanctuary. The most spectacular eskers in North America are also found on the upper Thelon.

When the Akiliniq Planning Committee released its draft management plan in 1996, David and I were surprised and excited by the committee's call for the establishment of two large special management areas adjacent to the sanctuary. These were to include the remainder of the Beverly herd's calving grounds as well as most, but not all, of the upper Thelon watershed. The special management areas would act as buffer zones to ensure the integrity of the sanctuary itself. They would enjoy some degree of protection, but mining activity would be permitted under special environmental controls. The committee also recommended a three-thousand-square-mile extension to the southwestern end of the sanctuary to include "an integral part of the ecological core of the sanctuary, which should receive the highest level of protection." The recom-

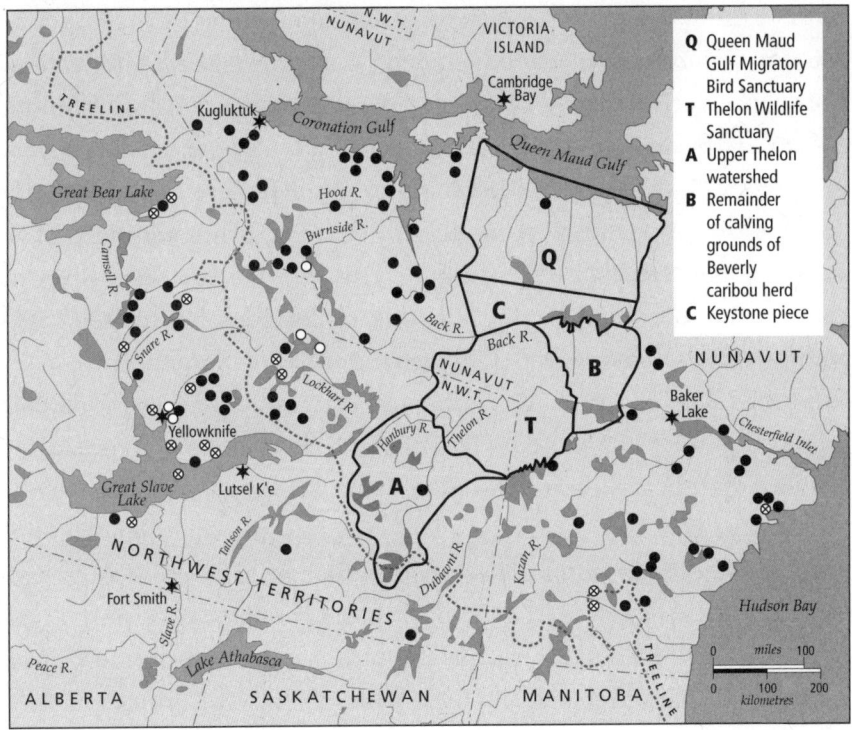

mendation for the creation of the two special management areas survived in a weakened and more vulnerable form in the final version of the management plan but, unfortunately, the plan has been delayed well past the July 1998 deadline required by the Nunavut land claim agreement. The necessary approvals from Nunavut to implement the management plan should be forthcoming very soon, but as of spring 2003 nothing was on the horizon for the NWT portion of the sanctuary.

The vision of the Akiliniq Planning Committee challenged David and me to think even bigger than we had dared to before. As a result, we expanded our proposal of areas that we believed should be protected from industrial development in the central Barrens to include both of the special management areas recommended by the committee. At a minimum, we concluded, our proposal should extend the conservation reach of the 13.8-million-acre Thelon Wildlife Sanctuary by adding all ten million acres of the upper Thelon watershed in the NWT and the remaining five million acres of the Beverly caribou herd's calving grounds in Nunavut. The addition of a keystone piece of about five million acres north of the Back River in Nunavut would ecologically link this entire complex to the 15.5-million-acre Queen Maud Gulf Migratory Bird Sanctuary, also in Nunavut. The result would be almost fifty million acres or 78,000 square miles of connected wildlands and wildwaters, protected for wildlife and the people who depend upon it forever.

An area this large would go a long way towards ensuring essential habitat for the future of arctic species that need to move over vast distances in order to survive. Our proposal would provide protection of critical wildlife habitat for the migratory caribou herds as a source of food for aboriginal peoples; for tundra wolves, wolverines and barren-ground grizzlies, which require extremely large home ranges; for staging, nesting and moulting areas of important bird colonies; and for the headwaters of the Thelon River—the largest watershed in the Barren Lands.

Our concept encompasses a spectacular, roadless wilderness stretching 450 miles, literally from treeline to tidewater. It would be the largest protected area in North America and one of the largest in the world—much larger than the maritime provinces of New Brunswick, Nova Scotia and Prince Edward Island combined, and many times larger than any other protected area in Canada. But as large as fifty million acres may sound, it represents only sixteen percent of the Barren Lands.

This idea's great practical strength is that existing conservation lands—the Thelon and Queen Maud sanctuaries—already make up nearly two-thirds of the central Barrens wilderness vision. Furthermore, northern aboriginal communities themselves have suggested most of the additional conservation lands which, along with the Thelon and Queen Maud sanctuaries, would fully recognize their traditional access, hunting, trapping and fishing rights. Indeed, this proposed conservation lands complex would be an effective way to protect access to subsistence hunting for the long term, both within and outside its boundaries, because these lands would serve as a "wildlife bank" for people in the surrounding areas. Also, this practical use of land, legally guaranteed, would give it sufficient value to compete with more disruptive industrial uses proposed in adjacent areas. Although there are no permanent communities within these proposed conservation lands, almost four percent of the area is Inuit Owned Land. All terms and conditions associated with such lands must be respected, of course, which could include dedication of these areas by Inuit for conservation purposes.

The big question for David and me now was, what were we going to do with this conservation vision? Obviously, it was going nowhere unless it was championed and moved forward by a consensus of northerners. The concept had to be transferred into the public arena, but our initial attempts to do so proved ineffective. Then, what seemed like the perfect vehicle to promote our ideas emerged from out of the blue—the decision by the federal and territorial governments to develop a "protected areas strategy" for the Northwest Territories with a "public conference" to be held in Inuvik in March 1997.

The NWT protected areas strategy arose out of the ashes of the federal environmental assessment review of the BHP diamond mine. World Wildlife Fund Canada had applied to the Federal Court for a judicial review of the entire process used to arrive at what World

Wildlife Fund viewed as the "disappointing and inadequate recommendations" of the environmental assessment panel that granted conditional approval to the BHP diamond mine. World Wildlife Fund wanted protected areas identified and reserved as a condition of the federal government's approval of the mine. Earlier, World Wildlife Fund had secured written commitments from the leaders of the provincial, territorial and federal governments to complete a network of protected areas representing all of the natural regions of Canada by the year 2000. The compromise reached for World Wildlife Fund to withdraw its Federal Court application was that the federal and territorial governments would develop a protected areas strategy for the NWT by 1998, announce three new arctic national parks and ensure that future federal environmental assessment procedures would be broad enough to include the cumulative ecological effects of development projects.

I saw the protected areas strategy conference in Inuvik as a unique opportunity, and I was determined to go. In fact, World Wildlife Fund, among others, encouraged me to attend and prepare a presentation on the central Barrens conservation vision that David and I were so excited about. According to World Wildlife Fund, the goal was to have the public advance as many candidates as possible for protected area status. However, I soon learned from the territorial government that this "public conference" wasn't open to the public after all. It was only open to the "stakeholders" invited by the territorial government—and they didn't consider me a legitimate stakeholder. The only way I could participate in the proceedings as a non-aboriginal was to attend as a delegate of one of the five conservation organizations on the invitation list. In the end, that was exactly how I got there.

The most encouraging part of the Inuvik conference was that the aboriginal delegates were clearly interested in protecting parts of their traditional lands from industrial development. However, I found the other aspects of the conference very disappointing. In the end, little was accomplished beyond establishing the ground rules under which geographic areas could be *considered* for the protected areas strategy. The most important of these ground rules stipulated that proposals for protected areas must originate with or be supported by the aboriginal communities or land claim groups in each region. This rule would apply in all regions, whether land claims had been settled there or not, and regardless of the fact that the vast majority of the North remained, and would always remain, publicly owned Crown land. While I recognized that the lead for the implementation of the strategy must come from the aboriginal population, I was disappointed that some kind of accommodation hadn't been made for non-aboriginal northerners like me to participate in the process in a direct and meaningful way. Along with the conservation organizations, over half the population of the NWT was relegated to the sidelines as spectators or facilitators at best.

Another disappointing development of the Inuvik conference was that delegates from the future territory of Nunavut failed to appear. The Inuit declared that their land claim supersedes all other processes and contains adequate provisions to create protected areas in Nunavut. With no opportunity for anyone at the conference to advance specific proposals for protected areas, I took advantage of the occasion to make sure every delegate in Inuvik received a written copy of the conservation vision for the central Barren Lands that David and I were promoting. Later, I also mailed copies to the Nunavut delegates who had boycotted the conference. My goal was to get our ideas out in the open and stimulate people to start talking about them and perhaps take some ownership of them. It's still an open question what impact our proposal has had on anyone in the North, but it did influence the thinking of one very important Canadian—Monte Hummel, president of World Wildlife Fund Canada.

Like myself, Monte was one of Doug Pimlott's students, but he came along after I had graduated. I didn't meet Monte until September 1978, when he gave a stirring eulogy at Doug's memorial service at the University of Toronto. That fall, we hunted ducks together on my farm with our mutual friend Dennis Voigt. I didn't see Monte again until the BHP diamond mine hearings in Yellowknife in February 1996. There, a bond was forged between us and, shortly after that, I started pestering him about the conservation concept for the central Barrens that David and I wanted to move forward. Admittedly, it didn't take much convincing to win Monte over to the practicalities of this idea. In Monte, David and I soon found a committed believer. As a result, our fifty-million-acre central Barrens conservation vision became a top priority in World Wildlife Fund Canada's long-term conservation plan. By the beginning of the new millennium, Monte was delegating some of his Toronto office responsibilities so that he would have enough time to assume the lead role in pursuing what he acknowledged could be "the biggest single conservation project in the history of Canada."

As anyone who has ever met him can confirm, Monte has charisma to spare, and in no time at all, it seemed, he had raised a large sum of money from a handful of supporters to begin conservation work in the central Barren Lands. Since any initiatives to protect lands in the vicinity of the Thelon Wildlife Sanctuary rest firmly in the hands of the people of Lutsel K'e and Baker Lake, the funds that Monte has raised are needed to ensure that financial constraints do not stand in the way of the conservation aspirations of these two aboriginal communities. Lutsel K'e and Baker Lake have both welcomed

World Wildlife Fund's offer to assist them to achieve their dreams of protecting some of their traditional homelands from industrial development. Monte and his assistants Bill Carpenter in the NWT and John Laird in Nunavut have been working hard to help transform those dreams into reality. The funds contributed are being used by Lutsel K'e and Baker Lake to identify and inventory the natural and cultural values of candidate conservation lands, to support community workshops, for GIS mapping, for studies of traditional ecological knowledge, for the preparation of reports, videos and translations, and to meet the expenses of steering group meetings and the travel costs associated with all of this conservation work.

Representatives from both communities met again in Lutsel K'e in 2001 to reaffirm their commitment to the long-delayed Thelon management plan and to solicit the support of both territorial governments in finalizing the plan. Lutsel K'e has also identified a study area of almost 24,000 square miles extending west from the Thelon sanctuary, within which it intends to make specific proposals for the NWT protected areas strategy. Another study area connected with the strategy could be established farther south as a result of planned meetings between Lutsel K'e and the Dene of Fond du Lac, Saskatchewan, whose traditional lands include the southernmost parts of the Thelon watershed in the NWT.

It's uncertain where all this will lead, but in the end it seems probable that there will be more protected areas in the central Barren Lands than there are now. Although the politics are complicated, a start has been made, and World Wildlife Fund is encouraging Lutsel K'e and Baker Lake to think big.

Canada is one of the few countries left in the world where citizens can still make choices concerning the future of large areas of wilderness. However, our options are shrinking with each passing year. Our country's remaining wilderness is under siege from oil, gas and hydroelectric development and from the mining, lumber and pulp and paper industries. Many ecologists have concluded that the choices we make in the next decade or two may well determine how much biological diversity persists over the next hundred, thousand or even million years.

The Canadian Arctic is one of the few places left on earth where a block of fifty million acres of virgin wildlands can be found. Large as that may seem, it is just six percent of the Northwest Territories and Nunavut. Only through the foresight and sheer determination of a coalition of northerners and other Canadians will an Eden this large be preserved intact for future generations. But we are running out of time. This is probably the last chance in the history of our nation to accomplish something of this magnitude. In another ten or fifteen years it may be too late.

Epilogue

Perhaps nowhere else on earth today can the immensity and purity of the wilderness be felt as it still can in the Barren Lands. For me, this is the most compelling part of the allure of this place. The nearest town or road is hundreds of miles away; you can travel across open country for weeks on end and never see a sign of modern man; you can still feel the primordial excitement of venturing into the unknown. Admittedly, it's become a lot harder in recent years to find that in many parts of the Barren Lands as the encroachments of industry push further north. But I remember travelling alone on the tundra in the 1970s, when I fairly leaped out of my sleeping bag each morning because I was so eager to experience what that day held in store for me. I had never felt so alive before in my life.

This is what it must have been like—this sense of freedom and space—looking out on the Great Plains 150 years ago. I don't think such feelings are possible in heavily forested country or in the mountains. I, personally, have the opposite kinds of feelings in those places. I feel hemmed in.

For those of us who grew up in the east, in places like southern Ontario, returning home is a shock: we can't believe that where we live is so small.

In the Barren Lands the scale is so gigantic, the open expanse of the land and sky so overwhelming, that you feel exposed, puny, powerless, vulnerable. It scares the hell out of some people! But it's good medicine to live for a while in a place where Mother Nature is so obviously in charge, where you do not feel powerful or important, where you feel reduced to a tiny, insignificant speck. I think we all need to feel more of this kind of humility and respect for our true place on planet Earth; it's good for the soul. So is travelling unarmed in country where grizzlies roam. It helps to keep you humble knowing there are animals out there that can tear you to pieces, even though they are rarely inclined to do so. The presence of grizzlies sharpens your senses and keeps you alert to your surroundings. You live a little closer to the way wild animals live in the company of their predators.

To me, the Barren Lands are the most beautiful and exciting place left on this earth. I have been privileged to know them when they were still wild and teeming with life. Like a bewitching mistress, the Barren Lands taught me how to love; they taught me how to hate. They fill my life with joy. There's not a day all winter long when I don't think of the Barren Lands. When I return to them each spring I feel like I am coming home.

The Barren Lands have become my religion, my church; they're sacred ground. I worship them. My soul is there. That is why my ashes will go there one day, so my body and spirit will remain part of the Barren Lands forever.

Index

Aberdeen Lake, 94, 159
aboriginal people. *See also* Dene;
   Inuit, 20
   artifacts of, 13
   decline in hunting by, 175–76
   as survivalists, 62
Addison, Ed, 27
Adlard, Harold (Hornby's camp mate),
   144, 148
Ahmek (Camp), Algonquin Park, 23,
   26–27
air clarity, declines in, 178
Akiliniq Planning Committee, 207–9
alder bushes, 33, 50, 161
Algonquin Park (Ontario). *See also*
   Ahmek Camp, 27, 65, 149
Anderson, Dr. R.M., 147
Antoniak, Kevin, 15, 76, 154–55
archaeology. *See* Barren Lands, archaeology of; spear points; Thelon River,
   archaeology of
Artillery Lake, 38, 146
aspen trees, 161, 169
Aylmer Lake, 40

Back, Sir George, 40, 180
the Back River, 40, 93, 98, 109, 121,
   180
Baffin Island, wolf research on, 27
Baker Lake, NWT, 28, 30, 159, 191–92,
   207, 214–15
balsam poplar trees, 161, 169
bannock, 14
Baron, Jack (memorable bush pilot),
   132–33
Baron, Joanne, 132

the Barren Lands, 19
   archaeology of, 83–85
   declining air clarity in, 178
   declining water clarity in, 178–79
   industrialization as a threat to,
      187–203, 206, 216
   lack of precipitation in, 60, 75
   naming of, 20
   pollution in, 82
   power of, 14, 22, 29, 217–18
   storms in. *See also* winds, 75–81
   temperatures in, 60, 76, 92, 142–43
   trappers in, 139–43
   vulnerability of the, 44, 216
Bathurst Inlet, 41, 45, 182, 194, 196
bears. *See* black bears; grizzly bears
beaver, 27, 162
The Beaver (HBC magazine), 28
berries (wild). *See also* raspberries, 171
Beverly Lake, 83, 85, 174
Big Esker Lake, 34–35, 102, 106
birch trees
   dwarf, 33, 39–41, 47–48, 160–61
   white, 71
birds, variety of in the Barren Lands, 21
Black, Richard (trapper & correspondent), 139–43
black bears, encounters with, 123–24,
   153–55
blackflies, 19, 38–39, 51, 75, 165
   canoeing and, 90–95
   cessation of, 41
Blanchet, Guy, 32, 146
Bloody Falls, 44
Bourque, Billy (memorable bush pilot),
   16, 133–36

Bourque, Jim, 191
Brace, Fred, 140
brant, 205
Bullock, James. *See* Critchell-Bullock
Burnside Falls, 51
the Burnside River, 45, 49, 177
"bushed," the stress of being, 72–73

campfires. *See* fires
Canada geese, 36, 157, 162, 167, 205
Canadian stroke (paddling). *See*
 Northwoods stroke
Canoe Arctic Inc., 30–31
canoeing. *See also* trips (canoe)
 advantages of, 64, 69
 paddling and, 65–68
caribou. (*See also photographic pages*),
 13, 141–42, 147
 blackflies and, 92–93
 early aboriginal hunting of, 20, 49
 encounters with, 38–39, 40–42,
  49–50, 126–27, 148, 163, 170
 herd names of, 162, 187
 injured, 167
 migrations of, 87–90
 numbers of, 21
 population changes in, 185–87
 threatened by industrial development, 201–2, 206–8
 trails made by, 20, 89
 wanderings of, 87
 winter census of, 127–28
Carpenter, Bill, 140–41, 215
Catling, Roger & Theresa (trappers),
 140–42
Central Barrens Conservation Vision,
 204–16
char, arctic, 43–44
Christian, Edgar (Hornby's cousin &
 diarist), 144, 148
Clarke, Dr. Doug (Hornby biographer),
 144–48
the Clarke River, 160, 164–65
Clinton-Colden Lake, 39
columbine, flowering, 161
Contwoyto Lake, 45–47, 49, 192,
 195–96
Coppermine, NWT. *See* Kugluktuk

the Coppermine River, 32–33, 40–44,
 47, 52, 108, 177
the Coronation Gulf, 192
cows, Herefords, 24
cranes, sandhill, 112, 205
Critchell-Bullock, Captain James
 (Hornby's friend), 146–48
currants (edible. *For* currents *see*
 rapids), 161

dams, for hydroelectric generation, 193–94
D'Aoust, Gus (trapper), 139–40
Dene (people). *See also* aboriginal people, 14, 40, 83–84, 146, 215
 hunting by, 37, 49
 fighting Inuit by, 44
 respect for wolves by, 99
Department of Indian Affairs and
 Northern Development, 190
Desteffany Lake, 46
diamond mines, 192–93, 197–98
the Diavik Mine, 195
disorientation. *See also* getting lost, 128
dogs. *See also* hounds; wolves
 huskies, 140–41, 154
Douglas, George (friend of Hornby),
 146–47
drumlins, 160
Drybone, Noel, 140
the Dubawnt River, 32–34, 37, 139
ducks, 25, 33, 36, 42, 46, 157, 167, 179

eagles, 1, 34, 51
 bald, 162, 167
 golden, 42, 162
the Ekati Mine, 195, 198
Elliot, Clive, 99
endurance, mental requirements for,
 63–64
eskers. (*See also photographic pages*),
 19–20, 33–35, 88–90, 101, 110, 119,
 139, 157, 159, 164, 208
 described and defined, 159
the Ethen-eldili River, 32, 35
Eyeberry Lake, 208

falcons, peregrine, 13, 51, 112, 132,
 157, 162, 166, 171

falls. *See* waterfalls
farming, in Ontario, 24
Finnie, O.S., 146–47
fires
  camp, 58, 82
  pollution from, 82
  wild, 161, 172, 175, 177–78
fireweed, 171
firewood
  demands made for more, 57–58
  good availability of, 47–48
  scarcity of, 39, 47
fish, eating of, 13
fishing, results of, 42–43
Fort Reliance, NWT, 139–40
Fort Smith, NWT, 31
foxes, 126
  arctic, 141–43, 146–47
  red, 171
Franklin, Sir John, 32, 49
Frobisher Bay, NWT. *See* Iqaluit
Funk, Dick, 133

Garnet Falls. (*See also* photographic pages), 169
Gates, Cormack, 15, 127, 186
geese. *See also* Canada geese; snow geese, 34, 205
getting lost, 71–72
gnats, 35
gold mining, 192, 195–97
Goldstein, Barry & Fred (client benefactors), 148
goon-stroke (paddling), 67
grayling, 34
Great Slave Lake, 31, 45, 139, 192
Griffiths, Peter, 94
grizzly bears. (*See also* photographic pages), 13, 21, 36, 95, 104, 147, 157, 163
  dens of, 110
  encounters with, 107–9, 111–15, 118–19, 163, 172, 173
  expanding numbers of, 180–81, 187
  expanding ranges of, 175
  humility encouraged by, 218
  predation by, 87, 167, 183

guiding
  leadership role necessary for, 59–60
  planning for, 54–55
  rigors of, 53
gulls, 167
Gunn, Anne, 15, 186
gyrfalcons, 13, 157, 162, 170–71

Hall, Evan (author's son), 31, 150–52, 154–55
Hall, Graham (author's son), 31, 150–52, 154–55
Hall, Helen & Jane (author's sisters), 23
Hanbury, David, 40, 180
the Hanbury River. *See also* maps (illustrated), 28, 32, 38, 68, 139, 146, 164
hare, arctic, 141, 147
Hawkings, Bob, 63, 125
hawks, rough-legged, 112, 171
Hearne, Samuel, 40, 44, 49, 99, 180, 200
Hoffman, Karl, encounters a bear, 152–53
the Hood River, 51, 177
Hornby, John (legendary pioneer), 144–48
Hornby Point (Thelon River), 148, 169–70
the Horton River, 177
hounds, Redbone, 26
Hudson Bay, 40
Hummel, Monte, 13–17, 214
hunting. *See also* ducks; raccoons, 26
  boyhood pleasures of, 25

ice (lake), 33, 38, 45–49
industrialization and the loss of wilderness, 187–203
Inuit (people) *See also* aboriginal people, 83–84, 192, 194–95, 211
  encounters with, 44
  1771 massacre of, 44
inuksuit (large human likenesses), 84
Iqaluit, Nunavut, 27
Ivanhoe Lake, 34
Izok Lake, mineral discoveries around, 194

jackpine trees, 177
jaegers, 36, 46, 48
Jonsson, Ragnar (trapper), 139
J-stroke (paddling), 66

the Kazan River, 37, 177
Kelly, Jonah, 117–18
Kelsall, John, 163, 172
Kendall River, 43
Kugluktuk, 29, 32, 193, 196
Kuyt, Ernie, 37

Lac de Gras, 45, 195
Laird, John, 215
Lake Bernard, 25
Lake Providence, 45–46
land, importance of respect for the, 81–83
lemmings, 147
lightning, 177
Lloyd, Hoyes, 146–47
the Lockhart River, 32–33, 38–39, 42, 45
longspurs, Lapland, 46
loons, 46, 76
    red-throated, 36, 167
loss of all direction (being lost). See getting lost
Luebbert, Lance (trapper), 139–41
the Lupin Gold Mine, 192, 195
Lutsel K'e, NWT, 207, 214–15
Lynx Lake, 139, 141–43

Mackenzie Valley Pipeline Project, 28
Mackinnon, Stu, 115
MacLean (clan of), 24
Magrum, George (trapper), 139
"Mandy" (not always a happy camper), 136–38
maps (illustrated)
    of the Barren Lands, 2–3
    of the central Barrens conservation vision, 209
    of major mineral deposits, 196
    of 1973 trip to Kugluktuk, 43
    of 1976 trip to Bathurst Inlet, 43
    of the Thelon Oasis area, 160–61

martens, 141
the Mary Frances River, 32–33, 37–38
Matonabbee (Chipewyan leader), 180, 200
merlins, 169
military flights, low level over wilderness, 189
minerals. See also Northern Mineral Policy
    explorations for, 31, 39, 52, 162, 176
    mining of. See also mining, 188–89, 191–99
mining. See maps (illustrated); minerals, mining of
mink, 141
moose, 13, 36, 42, 96, 154, 158, 162
    encounters with, 163, 166, 168, 170, 173
    expanding numbers of, 21, 187
    expanding ranges of, 175, 179
mosquitoes, 34–35
    canoeing and, 90–92, 94
    cessation of, 41
Mulroney, Brian, 188
Murphy, Matt (trapper), 139
muskoxen. (See also photographic pages), 13, 96, 143, 146–47, 158
    encounters with, 50–51, 105–7, 148, 163, 168, 170–72
    endangered status of, 162, 175, 181–83, 187
    expanding ranges of, 175
    population sizes of, 21, 110
    rare variety of, 206

Northern Mineral Policy (1986), 188
Northwest Territories, 19
Northwest Territories Wildlife Federation, 190
Northwoods stroke (paddling), 66
"no-trace" camping, 81
Nunavut, 19
    financial interests in development by, 194–95

Ottawa, ON, as a confining big city, 29
otters, 162
    new breeding ranges of, 179

paddling technique. *See* canoeing, paddling and; goon-stroke; J-stroke; Northwoods stroke
the Peacock Hills, 48–49
Pelly, David, 15–16, 163, 204, 206–13
Pelly, Laurie, 204
peregrine falcons. *See* falcons, peregrine
Pimlott, Dr. Douglas, 23, 26–27, 214
pingos, 172
plovers, 167, 205
Point Lake, 41
pollution, 82
porcupines, 162
Powder, Dave, encounters a bear, 153–54
Pritchett, Carolyn, 15, 51, 109 *(See also photographic pages)*
Pritchett, Jay, 15, 45, 51, 109 *(See also photographic pages)*
prospectors
 signs of past, 39, 48
 signs of recent, 52
"Protected Areas Strategy" proposal, 211–13
ptarmigan, willow, 36, 48, 147

quartzite (chipped), 84, 169
Queen Maud Gulf, 181–82
Queen Maud Gulf Migratory Bird Sanctuary, 204–11

raccoons, hunting of, 26
the Radford River, 164
rapids, 43
 blackflies and, 91
 dangers of, 70–71
 lining/wading up, 46
 navigable, 34–35, 44, 50
 requiring portages, 35, 46, 49, 51
raspberries, 161
ravens, wiliness of, 115–17
Riddle, Fred (bounty hunter/trapper), 116, 139
roads, as the death of wilderness areas, 193–94, 197–99
"Robert" (client used to taking charge), 56–59
robins, 36

Ruttan, Lia, 17, 31, 90, 103, 112, 128, 150–52, 154–55
Ruttan, Vern, 63–64

safety
 importance of, 70–71, 74–75
 learning of, 52
sanctuaries in the Barren Lands. *See* maps (illustrated); central Barrens conservation vision
sandhill cranes. *See* cranes, sandhill
sandpipers, 167, 205
scoters, 33, 36
the Shield (Canadian/Precambrian), 20, 25, 49, 64, 75, 134, 159, 164, 205
Slave Geological Province, 192–93, 196
sledding, with a canoe, 48–49
smallpox, 176
Smart Lake, 39
snow geese, 28, 205
songbirds, declining numbers of, 179
spear points (archaeological artifacts), 169
splash covers on canoes, 68
spruce trees. *(See also photographic pages)*, 20, 33, 35–36, 38, 40, 83, 101–2, 140, 157, 159–60, 164, 172, 177, 180
 black, 77–78
 white, 42, 122, 150, 161, 166–67, 169
squirrels
 arctic ground, 36, 42, 50, 147
 red, 36, 162, 179
Stewart, Allan (trapper), 145
"stone men" (steering ancient caribou), 83
storms. *See* Barren Lands, storms in
strokes (paddling). *See* goon-stroke; J-stroke; Northwoods stroke
swans, tundra, 42, 167, 205

tamarack trees, 159
terns, arctic, 46, 167
Thelon Canyon, 165
the Thelon River. *See also* maps; *and, photographic pages*, 28, 32, 36–37, 52, 67–68, 72, 84, 90, 102, 104–5, 110–11, 126, 139, 144, 146, 177

224   INDEX

archaeology of, 163–64
description of, 158–74
Heritage River status of, 159
Thelon Wildlife Sanctuary, 147, 161–62, 181–82, 204, 206–11
    threatened loss of protections to, 188–92
Thompson, George (Margot's blind husband), 131–32
Thompson, Margot, 131–32
Thorpe, Ron, 28
thunderstorms, 38
tourism (business), early status of in NWT, 29–30
trappers, decline in hunting by, 175
the treeline, 20, 40, 45, 49, 70–72, 88, 92–93, 96, 139, 150, 158–59, 161, 181–82, 184, 205, 210
trees. See specific exemplars of (e.g. birch trees)
trips (canoe)
    rigors of, 60–62
    social psychology of, 55–61
trout, 25
    "aggression" by, 173
Trytten, Terry (bush pilot), 151
Tyrrell, J.W., 32, 37–38, 40, 180

Urangesellschaft Canada, 192
uranium
    demand levels for, 204
    open pit mining of, 192
Ursus Islands (Thelon River), 111, 160, 165, 170, 173–74

Voigt, Dennis, 27, 29, 32, 52, 61, 115, 214
voles, 96

Waldron, Malcolm (Hornby biographer), 147–48
water clarity, declines in, 178–79
waterfalls. See also named falls (e.g. Bloody Falls), 44

Whalley, George (Hornby biographer), 144
White Wolf Lake, 35, 116
widgeons, 42
Wilberforce Falls. (See also photographic pages), 51
wilderness, untouched, 22
wildflowers, 13, 19
the Willingham Hills, 48
willows, 24, 33, 40, 47, 50, 102, 110, 157, 160, 167–68, 172, 180
winds, 19
    severe and inhibiting, 38, 80–81
wolverines, 21, 95, 107, 163, 175, 187
    encounters with, 120–22
    as an index species, 121
    threatened by industrial development, 206
wolves. (See also photographic pages), 13, 21, 50, 143, 146–47, 157, 163
    colours of, 96
    dens of, 97, 100–102
    encounters with, 37, 39, 48, 100, 102–5, 148–50, 163, 166, 170–71, 173
    the howling of, 23, 26, 101, 128, 149
    hunted by humans, 184–85
    personalities of, 95, 97–99
    poisoning of, 116, 183–85
    population numbers of, 175
    predation by, 87, 167
    rearing practices of, 97
    research on, 27
    social organization of, 95–96
    threatened by industrial development, 206
World Wildlife Fund, 211–12, 214–15
Wray, Gordon, 191

Yamba Lake, 46
Yellowknife, NWT, 28–31, 194